Energy Is

Therefore

God Could Be

Modern Science Refutes Atheism

"Let There Be Light"
Was Not Just Poetry

Patrick Daniel McGrath

Copyright

Cover image credit NASA / WMAP Team   https://map.gsfc.nasa.gov

In-text image enhancement using convert.town and fotor.com

Printed by CreateSpace, An Amazon.com Company

Library of Congress Control Number: 2017914686

Publisher's Cataloging-In-Publication Data
(Prepared by The Donohue Group, Inc.)

Names: McGrath, Patrick D. (Patrick Daniel), 1954-
Title: Energy is therefore God could be : modern science refutes atheism / Patrick Daniel McGrath.
Description: 1st edition paperback. | Overland Park, KS : P.D.McGrath, [2017] | "'Let there be light' was not just poetry."--Cover. | Includes bibliographical references and index.
Identifiers: ISBN 978-1-9757-1380-5 (paperback) | ISBN 1-9757-1380-X (paperback)
Subjects: LCSH: Religion and science. | Atheism. | God--Proof. | Force and energy--Religious aspects--Christianity.
Classification: LCC BL240.3 .M34 2017 | DDC 201.65--dc23

With Correction of Typos Per Reader Input Through 12/26/17 and Feb 2020

Deus verus est

Acknowledgements

I thank those who helped shape the progressive drafts of this manuscript. Thank you Ken, Eric, Katie, Erin, Jason, Dan, and Kelly for your feedback. I thank readers in the early days of October through December 2017 for additional editorial input. Thank you Tawnya for shaping raw ideas into a meaningful cover.

Dedication

I dedicate this work to Kathy, my wife. You are my most vital source of inspiration, a wise and calm voice in times of worry, the answer to my prayer in times of doubt, and my best friend in times of joy. I thank God for you, Kathleen.

Table of Contents

Preface

I am a scientist who believes in God. Unfortunately, I know from direct and indirect means that derisive criticism can be expected by anyone who publicly claims to be a scientist who believes in God. A new breed of highly combative atheists aggressively claims that God has been disproven by modern science and they will take to task any who disagree with their worldview.

As a college freshman, I was advised by a recent graduate to expect that advanced scientific coursework would refute the foundations of my faith. Through both undergraduate and graduate training, I found that this was an increasingly common opinion. For decades, I've remained open to the arguments for both the atheist and the theistic views of this world. I've continued to pursue knowledge both within and beyond my primary area of scientific work. What I have found is the complete absence of any scientific fact that served as evidence against God. Instead, the more I learned about science the more I found nature behaving in ways that are fully consistent with faith. As I reach the end of a career, it is time to share my observations of the interface between science and faith.

What I have found is that a small but vocal group of highly aggressive atheists are actively engaged in the opposition to faith in the existence of God, any God. These are not people who express various levels of doubt, but people who express complete opposition to God. They do not believe in God and they want no one else to believe in God. They write books, present lectures, shape television documentaries and control the content of elementary science textbooks in the unbridled opposition to the popular expression of faith. Today's highly aggressive atheist charges that it is impossible to understand modern science and still believe in God. They charge that faith in God is a byproduct of scientific ignorance and superstition. The truth is that aggressive atheists are wrong.

Today's highly aggressive atheists misrepresent the facts of science. They mislead those who fail to check the facts. In this book we will check the facts and will see that the existence of a creative God remains fully consistent with the facts of modern science. Specifically, we will see that the God of the Bible is fully consistent with modern science.

If the question of whether God exists or not remained limited to the personal choice of faith, this topic would not be worth the effort spent in support of this book. However, the atheistic movement today is not simply about formation of individual opinion. The current atheistic movement pursues the elimination of all religion, and that makes it worthy of close study. Our children represent the primary social target for bringing about this change. The targeting of our children elevates this topic to my highest priority.

Breaking the link between parents and children is seen as the critical strategy for bringing about the elimination of religion from western society. Teaching of religion by parents to children is now commonly characterized by active atheists as a form of child abuse. Strident activism directed against religion of any denomination makes it critical to examine the basis upon which atheism attempts to prevail. Those with a deep understanding of scripture will understand that, in the long run, a widespread rejection of faith will indeed become very popular within this world. A critical question is whether you choose to be personally swept into that dynamic.

The rise of popular atheism is ironic because the preponderance of modern scientific evidence actually supports faith in God more so than atheism. The dynamic that is underway today is not based upon fact, logic, or reason. In truth, the atheistic dynamic is illogical, unreasonable and not based upon fact. In this book, we will review the foundations of science that relate to the plausibility of a creative God as described in the Bible. We will drill into the factual details. We will find that faith is not a byproduct of ignorance. Faith in God is a reasonable paradigm for life in this modern day and age.

Arguments of atheists include two general types of attack. First, atheists claim that those who believe in God are ignorant of scientific fact. They claim that the concept of God was invented by ignorant humans in order to explain the mechanisms for natural events in our world. Since science can now explain the mechanisms for many physical processes, atheists argue that God is no longer a necessary invention. Secondly, atheists rail against the many flaws and failures of organized religion. They argue that the proliferation of many religions and the public failures of the faithful reflect the absence of a good God.

That paired attack might sound like a strong argument but it is not. We will find that the arguments of the active atheist are simply not justified by the facts of science. It is true that modern science reveals many details of the mechanisms of action for this universe. However, knowledge of scientific detail regarding mechanisms of action is not evidence of the absence of a creative God. It is also true that organized religion is guilty of many flaws and failures throughout history, including real failures in our current day. However, the sins of humans, even religious humans, are not evidence of the absence of God.

One defense against atheistic logic involves the close examination of the two-fold attack against religion. It is charged that humanity has invented God to support basic human wants and needs. It is also charged that we fail miserably in our obedience to the God we invented. Together that pair of assertions illustrates the logical failure of the atheist argument. Logic would demand that a God invented by humanity would be closely matched to our wants and whims. Where is the logic in the expectation that humans have invented a God that drives us to achieve that which we do not want to achieve? That is simply not logical. That is not reasonable.

That said, this book is not a collection of arguments structured upon linguistic exercises of logic and reason. This book is intended for those who want a very close look at the data-driven interface between scientific fact and religious faith. We will look closely at those topics of modern science that relate most directly to the possibility or plausibility of God. Fortunately, this does not require that we all become elite scientists. An effective mid-level understanding of the relevant topics is possible even for those, like myself, who are not elite. This understanding will, however, require that we tackle some basic math. Be assured that this math is within our reach. While the original discovery of scientific facts often required elite mathematical skills, a working understanding of established science can be achieved using basic algebra within the reach of every high school student. In return for the effort, this math will provide the reader with a very deep understanding of some of the most important discoveries of the 20th century.

Chapter 1. Atheism Is On the Attack

David Silverman is the president of American Atheists, the group founded by Madelyn Murray O'Hair. This is the group that brought about the court-ordered removal of prayer from U.S. public schools in the 1960s. This same group has recently pioneered the posting of anti-faith billboards during Christmas and other religious holiday periods. In his book, _Fighting God_, [1] Silverman makes clear that his expressed goal is to 'wipe out' religion - all religion. One of the most chilling of the tactics expressed by Mr. Silverman is the introduction of the concept that the teaching of religion to children by parents is a form of child abuse. He is not alone in this effort.

Silverman is joined by Christopher Hitchens[2] (God is Not Great; How Religion Poisons Everything), Richard Dawkins[3] (The God Delusion), Sam Harris [4] (_The End of Faith; Religion, Terror and the Future of Reason_ and _Letter to a Christian Nation_) and others in a proliferation of work attacking any and all religious faiths. These atheistic leaders join in a common characterization of the teaching of faith to children as a form of child abuse. In a coordinated fashion, these atheistic leaders call for social change that would prohibit any teaching of faith until adulthood. Their shared goal is the isolation of children from the teachings of the parent. The ultimate goal is the achievement of the demise of faith within a single generation. This is not my interpretation of their goals or their tactics; this is their own description of goals and tactics.

The level of hatred and vitriol toward those of faith is unmistakable when the work of these authors is studied using the audibly narrated

---

[1] Silverman, David. Fighting God; An Atheist Manifesto For a Religious World New York, Thomas Dunne Books, St. Martin's Press, 2015 ISBN. 9781250064844

[2] Hitchens, Christopher. God is Not Great; How Religion Poisons Everything New York, Warner 12, 2007 ISBN 9780446579803

[3] Dawkins, Richard The God Delusion Boston, Houghton Mifflin Co., 2006 ISBN 978061868009

[4] Harris, Sam. The End of Faith; Religion, Terror and the Future of Reason New York: W. W. Norton & Co., 2004 ISBN 9780393327656 and Harris, Sam. Letter to a Christian Nation New York: Knopf, 2006 ISBN 9780307265777

versions of their books. Although atheism is technically the absence of religion, the atheistic movement today acts with the organized energy and emotional fervor of a zealous religious movement. The active atheist movement today is a type of jihad with complete intolerance for any and all expressions of faith in God.

It is important to look at the mechanisms through which this antagonism toward faith is prosecuted. This is important whether you started reading this book from a foundation of pre-existing faith or not. If you are a fair-minded person interested in the pursuit of truth and justice, you will want to know whether those who pursue restrictions on the faithful are truthful or not. It is important to understand the mechanisms of the attack against faith so that you can examine whether that attack has merit.

One of the most common forms of attack against faith is the dissemination of the message that faith is a byproduct of ignorance.

"Let me suggest that, whether or not heaven exists, Alexander sounds precisely how a scientist should not sound when he doesn't know what he is talking about."

That quote is drawn from the publicized attack of the account of a near death experience (NDE) personally suffered by a practicing neurosurgeon.[5,6] Sam Harris, one of the aggressive atheists referenced above, attacked the personal account of this fully trained physician without any direct involvement in his case. Harris had no direct data regarding Dr. Alexander's near-death experience. However, with aggression not supported by facts, Harris attacks the account of this NDEfor no reason other than a pre-judged opposition to the idea of God.

---

[5] Miller, Lisa: Discovering Heaven, p97 , Time Home Entertainment, Time Books, 2014
[6] Dr. Harris's criticism of Dr. Alexander's account of his personal near death experience. http://www.samharris.org/blog/item/this-must-be-heaven

"Their discomfort was fueled by the fact that few of these people could understand the content of the book, as virtually none of them had any scientific education and most were generally hostile to science on ideological grounds anyway.[7]"

This quote is derived from Paul Davies, an author of popular summaries of physics, who rose to the defense of Stephen Hawking. Hawking, arguably the most famous of all writers of popular science, routinely concludes that God does not exist while summarizing facts that could just as easily support a conclusion that God is very real. For this, Hawking regularly receives his fair share of criticism. In this case, Hawking absolutely deserved criticism. Hawking had proposed a concept in which additional dimensions of spacetime could be defined using a dimension of time valued using the imaginary numbers (square roots of negative numbers). As we will consider in a later chapter, this possibility argues as much for the possibility of God as against it. Hawking, like other atheistic scientists, is guilty of presenting the facts of the universe as though they support only the atheistic conclusion when the truth is that they equally well support faith in God and the construct of heaven as a separate realm. Hawking's one-sided reviews of science create false and misleading perceptions of what science says about faith. The misuse of high scientific credentials to mislead others deserves criticism. Those who understand why this criticism is deserved are not ignorant.

"You don't talk about the spherical earth with NASA and then say, let's give equal time to the flat-earthers.[8]"

Flat-earthers! To imply that those who believe in a Creator are as completely discredited as those who once argued that the earth was flat is wrong on multiple levels. That quote is from Neil deGrasse Tyson, the popular host of a number of televised summaries of science, including the series *COSMOS*. This Time Magazine quote

---

[7] Paul Davies, P184-185, Chapter 8, Imaginary Time, in <u>About Time, Einstein's Unfinished Revolution</u>, New York, Simon & Schuster, NY, 1995. ISBN 0671799649

[8] Quote from Neil deGrasse Tyson , Time Magazine, April 7, 2014

expressed the atheist's view that anyone who believes in a Creator is ignorant of the facts of science. As we progress through this book you will come to see that this is simply not the truth.

Pursuit of objectivity without editorial bias is a declared goal of the scientific method, but today's atheistic scientists do not reflect that ethic. It is wrong to slant the truth when purporting to teach a dispassionate summary of scientific facts. It is especially wrong when the biased presenter flaunts high academic credentials that are expected to reflect a commitment to the truth – the whole truth.

The biggest problem with active atheism is not the slinging of insults but the current pursuit of social marginalization and restriction of faith-based opinions. One of the many popular web sites purporting to discuss the various arguments in support of atheism presented the following interpretation of the US Constitution language addressing religion.

> The principle of the separation of church and state is that the state shall not legislate concerning matters of religious belief. In particular, it means not only that the state cannot promote one religion at the expense of another, **but also that it cannot promote any belief which is religious in nature**.[9] (emphasis added)

The bolded portion of that quote is not unique to a single web blogger, but is a common theme among atheistic activists. This additional limitation is a complete perversion of what the US constitution actually says. The original and historic interpretation of the Constitution is that any person should be allowed to participate as a holder of office or as an engaged citizen regardless of how that person derives the personal sense of what is right and what is wrong. I should be free to fully participate in the public discourse even if my interpretation of "right from wrong" differs from those who adhere to an atheistic viewpoint. However, the practical reality is that active

---

[9] http://infidels.org/library/modern/mathew/intro.html (viewed October 26, 2015)

atheists are working to reshape social opinion in ways that bring their extreme interpretation into play as the ruling authority in this and other nations. It is important to remember that similar examples of legalized oppression of religion have happened before. In each case, it took less than a single generation to bring about the legal marginalization of the faithful.

To understand the foundations for atheism today, it is important to review the historical basis for the association of atheism with scientific training. One will find that there were data-driven reasons why 19th century scientists were convinced that a Creator was impossible. We will also find that the reason for this belief was fully reversed as the 20th century unfolded. Atheism in the sciences today is outdated by more than 100 years of factual progress. Today, atheism continues as a matter of enforced indoctrination, not as a function of scientific fact.

Overt strife between science and religion took shape in the 17th century. The original conflict was over the issue of whether the sun orbited around the earth or whether Earth orbited the sun. The Catholic Church insisted that the Bible taught that the earth was fashioned in a completely immobile position, supported by physical pillars. The Church insisted that the earth was orbited by the sun and the stars. The Church believed this because of an overly-literalistic interpretation of scripture. The Catholic Church was wrong.

Galileo Galilei had confirmed the work of his elder, Copernicus, and began to teach that the earth and other planets orbited the sun. This was in direct opposition to the teachings of the Church. In those days the Church also held powers of state and that power was often used without wisdom. Galileo was threatened with excommunication unless he reversed his position. Galileo changed his position only partially and only temporarily. For this, he was sentenced to house arrest by the Roman Catholic Church-state.

Chapter 1

The Catholic censorship and punishment of Galileo and others were wrong and permanently harmful in many ways. Among other harm, this error triggered a formalized opinion that science and religion are inherently in conflict. It set the stage for the presumption that science is right and religion is wrong. The Galileo affair was a powerful factor in the response of the scientific community to the next important conflict between religion and science.

Starting in the 17th century, advancements in physics established the basis for expecting that neither energy nor matter could be created nor destroyed. By the late 18th century, the principles of conservation were considered inviolable laws of physics. If matter cannot be created, then the earth and heavens could not be created. The story of a Creator seemed completely debunked by the facts of science. This led to a significant shift toward atheism by scientists of that day. By the end of the 19th century, almost all leaders of the scientific elite publicly espoused atheism as their personal worldview.

As the 20th century dawned, Einstein's theory of relativity reversed the 19th century understanding of the laws of conservation. The foundation for the only scientific argument ever directed against faith in our Creator was completely reversed. Einstein taught the world that matter could be formed from no prior matter through transformation of pure energy. As such, the conservation laws apply strictly to energy and not to matter. Energy can neither be created nor destroyed, but matter can come and go through interconversion with pure energy. A creation event does not violate the known laws of physics. A creation event is possible, therefore our Creator is possible. As the 20th century progressed, multiple avenues of scientific measurements consistently added new evidence for the plausibility of God.

With the reversal of the misunderstanding that represented the foundation of 19th century atheism, one might have expected a quick reversal of attitude. In defiance of pure logic, this reversal has not happened. Today, nothing but irrational bias supports the continued adoption of atheism by those who would like to think of themselves as intellectually elite. The mechanism that allows this bias to continue is the highly subjective process for recruitment, training, and funding of each new generation of scientists. The enriched voice of atheism established in the 19th century continues simply because those who want to be elite work hard to emulate the genius, Albert Einstein. Einstein never retreated from his atheistic worldview, and it takes a strong mind to move away from his example.

Albert Einstein trained in the late 19th century and he fully embraced atheistic views of the world. Although he spoke of God in discussion of science, this was only his euphemism for 'the forces of nature.' Even though his work reversed the one and only strong argument against faith in a Creator, Einstein remained a committed atheist. Many of Einstein's ardent admirers continue to emulate Einstein's public persona including the public support for atheism. However, this worldview is no longer based upon fact. Atheism continues today as an example of enforced groupthink.

While there is no longer any fact of science that directly refutes belief in God, atheism remains the preference of the subset of scientists with the highest level of training. More than 85% of the National Academy of Science identify a religious preference of 'atheism or not religious.' This is about three- to four-fold more prevalent than that same characterization from the US population at large. It is easy to misinterpret this dynamic, expecting that advanced scientific training reveals detailed facts that argue against God. That is absolutely not the case. The enrichment of atheists within this group of elite scientists is best explained by social dynamic more than scientific fact. This enrichment is the result of intergenerational transmission of atheism like any other religious choice. Atheism continues to be passed from the elder to the initiate through the processes of selection and reinforcement. Bias is stacked

11

in favor of selection of atheistic candidates for advancement to the highest ranks of academic tenure.

Membership in the National Academy of Science and the National Science Foundation is a matter of nomination and selective review. It is reasonable to expect that the prevalence of atheism might become enriched if there was active bias against the invitation and ratification of those who are known believers in God. The video record of statements of an elite scientist demonstrates that this type of selection bias is absolutely real. Speaking to a group of like-minded scientists, Dr. Neil deGrasse Tyson felt comfortable disparaging the potential contribution of those of faith engaged in science. Claiming that religion opposes the intellectual requirements for scientific pursuit, Dr. Tyson was explicit in his bias as follows:

"I don't want these guys in the lab – they won't solve problems." He goes on to declare his opinion that the real question is not why 85% of the National Science Foundation reject God, but why NSF still includes 15% membership that do not.[10]

Selection bias in the sciences is very real and this selection bias is not limited simply to membership in the National Science Foundation. It is important to understand that atheistic leadership has the right to select and groom like-minded students for advanced training programs. This selection bias is also important for the successful competition for research grant funding. Progression to the top ranks of any field of science is not guaranteed simply by making good grades in the fundamental science courses. Subjective assessments of "thinking ability" represent important criteria for admission into advanced science training programs. The comments of Dr. Neil deGrasse Tyson demonstrate that biased selection against those of

---

[10] Neil deGrasse Tyson https://www.youtube.com/watch?v=ASmQmYX-71Q viewed 08.26.14

faith is real. Subjective selection bias, not the facts of science, explains the exaggerated concentration of atheists within the ranks of scientific leaders today.

It is important to know this. Faced with the fact that the majority of elite scientists profess atheism, it is easy for the lay person to simply capitulate to the expectation that these experts must know something that argues against faith. That is simply not the truth! The high proportion of atheists in the scientific community reflects nothing other than a biased selection process. Atheists are more prevalent in the ranks of elite scientists because atheists continue to favor atheists for selection and advancement.

Bias in favor of the atheist opinion also shapes the decision to select or reject various academic papers for publication. A relevant example is the furor caused by the 2004 publication of a review article that was subsequently criticized because its conclusions did not support the atheistic interpretation of evolution. Stephen C. Meyer Ph.D. submitted and received peer-review clearance for his review of the existing literature describing primary knowledge of the proliferation of new life forms during the Cambrian Explosion (a brief period of emergence of new animal species at a rate faster than at any prior or later time in natural history) [11].

Using the science of information theory, Dr. Meyer assessed the degree to which the ordering of DNA information could be characterized as simple or complex (random vs. non-random). The more non-random information is, the stronger the signal for a preexisting intelligence with advanced awareness of whether intermediate changes would yield benefit or not. This topic relates to the possible resolution of the question of whether Darwinian evolution is a process that is exclusive or inclusive of a creative God.

---

[11] **Meyer, Stephen C,** The origin of biological information and the higher taxonomic categories, Proceedings of the Biological Society of Washington 117(2):213-239. 2004

Atheistic interpretation of Darwin's work requires a conclusion that evolution happens without a creative intelligence. Those who believe in God expect that a creative intelligence can be observed in the processes of nature. This dichotomy can be studied scientifically by measuring the degree of randomness for documented DNA changes. Higher degrees of random distribution support the atheistic viewpoint. Lower degrees of random distribution support the idea of the involvement of pre-existing awareness. Meyer's review article demonstrated that the factual record of nature is statistically less random than one would expect from strictly materialistic processes alone. His conclusion was that the period known as the Cambrian Explosion reflected patterns of change consistent with a cosmic intelligence demonstrating advance awareness of the relative merits of optional combinations of individual changes.

In the short interval between the publication of Meyer's article and publication of the subsequent issue of that monthly scientific journal, the atheistic community mounted an outraged response. The editor that authorized the publication of Meyer's article was immediately dismissed by his superiors. Cowing to the pressure of the atheistic response, the journal leadership published a retraction and repudiation of Meyer's article. The executive leadership claimed that the dismissed editor had approved this paper for publication without the required preliminary peer review.

The attacks against that editor were shown to be false. The dismissed editor publicly defended his actions, rejecting the journal's characterization of his actions as those of a lone wolf. This story was picked up by major news organizations including the Wall Street Journal, other major news outlets, and it received the attention of a U.S. federal oversight committee. The conclusion was that the leadership of the journal had falsely accused the editor of wrongdoing. The truth was that the article had been reviewed by three independent peer review authorities, just as required. The peer reviewers' comments were consistent with acceptance of Meyer's work as a worthy contribution to the scientific literature.

In the aftermath of that resolution, the atheist community has publicly called for a consensus among peer reviewers to work against the publication of "antievolutionist" manuscripts. Eugenie Scott, executive director of the National Center for Science Education, is a pronounced and active atheist. She is a leader in the call for this type of scientific censorship. She has publicly urged peer review referees to reject any manuscript that could be perceived as antievolutionist. All it takes to be antievolutionist is to report any finding that suggests that the world works in any way that is statistically different from the purely materialistic patterns expected by atheism.

The prejudgment against any paper that disagrees with the materialistic interpretation of evolution demonstrates a corruption of the scientist's commitment to pursue truth no matter where that leads. Active atheism of this type is not logical science; it is a program of propaganda under the guise of science.

Atheistic opinions within the scientific community are no longer simply the reflection of individual choices. Atheism has become a self-reinforced call for compliance and message control. In a system of tenure intended to support the unfettered pursuit of truth, thought control has returned. Today differs from the days of Galileo with regard to the source and direction of the imposition of thought control. Today the corrupting forces do not originate from outside, but act from within the scientific community. The direction of the prejudice is now directed squarely against faith, with the insistence that science must enforce a strictly materialistic worldview.

The irony is that while atheistic activism has never been more aggressive, the scientific facts supporting atheism have never been weaker. With atheism so aggressively supported by leading scientists, I expected that my graduate level training would reveal facts that explain the atheistic rationale. I found the opposite. I found that atheism has not been supported by favorable evidence since the correction of the 19th century misunderstanding of the conservation laws.

Since the beginning of the 20th century, the facts of science have steadily reinforced reasons to believe in our Creator. Today, we know that matter can be created from no prior matter. Furthermore, we know that is exactly what happened. Science knows that this world really is something made from nothing. This world is a collection of matter derived from a pool of raw material that originally held no matter, no space, and no time. This is fully supportive of faith in God as described in the Genesis scriptures.

The only current argument held by science against the Bible is directed to the insistence that creation involved an interval of only six consecutive Earth days taking place only 10,000 years ago. That is an incorrect reading of scripture. While strict young-earth creationism reflects the view of only a minority of those who believe in our Creator, this interpretation of the Bible remains a favorite target for ridicule by atheists. This book will make the case that young-earth interpretation is, in fact, wrong. It is wrong scientifically and it is wrong theologically. It is simply not the truth and it is harmful because it brings the Bible to needless ridicule.

With respect for those who deeply believe that creation involved only six contiguous current Earth days, I can do nothing better than to refer the reader to the excellent work of John Lennox[12]. Dr. Lennox effectively describes the biblical basis upon which the days of Genesis scripture are correctly interpreted to represent the relative ordering of creation steps, not the duration of each step.

---

[12] Lennox, John C. Seven Days that Divide the World. The Beginning According to Genesis and Science Grand Rapids, MI., Zondervan, 2011. ISBN 9780310492177

The Bible must be read with respect for the cosmic scope of God, unbound by the myopic nature of mankind, and unbound by any measure of time. A day in Genesis should be understood as a systematic step-wise progression unbounded by time. Any specific day in Genesis Chapter 1 might consume any measure of current time ranging from a fraction of a second to millions of years in duration. The intervening 'evening and morning' reflected between these steps does not reflect the setting and rising of Earth's sun. These words reflect the progressive completion of one creative step before the beginning of the next. This is the "day-age" interpretation of the Genesis scriptures and this enjoys a solid theological foundation. It also reveals a perfect match between the ancient scriptures and the measurements of modern science. Those who stay with me throughout this book will see that the day-age interpretation is a truthful interpretation of scripture that vividly reveals the reality of God.

Upon completion of this book, rejection of faith might still be held as one's personal choice, but this choice cannot be defended as the only logical option in the face of modern science. The truth is that the facts of modern science do not refute faith. They refute atheism.

Chapter 2. Energy Is Therefore God Could Be

Atheists argue that God makes no sense in light of modern science, but they cannot point to any fact that directly refutes the possibility of God. On the other hand, scientific progress of the 20th and 21st centuries has strengthened scientific evidence which is consistent with faith in God as revealed in the Bible. The only fact-based argument ever mounted by science against faith completely crumbled during the 20th century. Atheists hang on today only as a matter of their own type of faith which is simply a personal antagonism toward God. For this antagonism, they have no factual support.

Richard Dawkins, author of _The God Delusion_, is one of today's most outspoken atheists. He is one of those who teaches that religion is harmful in all its forms. Dawkins actively preaches that religions of all creeds and denominations deserve direct, public opposition. He is one of those atheists who stridently argue that the teaching of religion by parents to their children should be classified as child abuse. Dawkins exemplifies the modern atheist in the demonstration of confidence exceeding competence. He is absolutely wrong, but he is very confidently wrong.

When analyzed closely, the atheist's argument breaks down to nothing more than the presentation of a contrasting hypothesis, the null hypothesis. The atheistic argument does not include evidence against God. It simply assumes the absence of God. It is nothing more than a statement of belief – atheistic belief. This contrasting hypothesis does not rule out the possibility of God.

Richard Dawkins claims that the origin and maturation of our universe can be explained on the basis of uncomplicated processes that become progressively more complex through natural selection. He argues that God is not necessary to explain that process, therefore God is not real. This is a complete misrepresentation of the scientific method. Dawkins has presented nothing other than one hypothesis; one hypothesis out of two. It is true that we can propose explanations of the world that do not invoke God. However, the simple fact that we understand details of natural mechanisms is not evidence of the absence of our Creator. When challenged on this point, Dawkins simply asserts that those who disagree with his view are not intelligent enough to fully understand the concepts of natural selection.

The truth is that the principles and processes of natural selection are not terribly complex and the faithful can fully understand this area of science. We can understand it thoroughly and we can recognize that Darwinian evolution says nothing that factually argues against the possibility of God.

God has not been disproven by the current knowledge of Darwinian evolution for a couple of reasons. The first is that the drivers of change at each node of the 'tree of life' can be explained both with and without involvement of God. That is not different from any other unresolved scientific question. Both the null and alternative hypotheses remain viable until one is ruled out. Atheists may argue in support of their favored hypothesis but they have given no fact that rules out the possibility that God is real. The second limitation of evolution without the active leadership of God is that Darwin taught us nothing about how life originated from that which was not already alive. This is not a minor flaw today. A full 150 years have passed since this theory was originally taught. Since that time, mankind has discovered the phonograph and progressed to achieve high fidelity solid state electronics. We have discovered heavier-than air flight and progressed to supersonic aviation and interstellar exploration. We have converted the steam engine to internal combustion engines and cycled back to external heat engines in the form of the turbojet. We have learned how to touch individual cells to bring about *in vitro* fertilization. We have cloned sheep. We have engineered virgin birth in an animal as close to humans as the laboratory mouse. However, we have not been able to trigger even the most basic life without a seed that was already alive. The stark truth of Darwin's theory on the origin of life is that it teaches nothing about the origin of life. Darwin's observations might have relevance for the expression of biological diversity, but they do not rule out God as the author of life.

The only reason that atheism is associated with Darwin's work is that atheism was a presumption of the scientific community at the time of Darwin's work. Darwin proposed his theory during the mid-19th century when science mistakenly believed that matter could not be created. In Darwin's age, atheism had a data-driven reason to argue against the possibility of creation. It made sense at that time to examine the processes of life from a purely mechanistic viewpoint. Assuming the absence of a creator, Darwin sought and found a possible explanation for biologic diversity. However, during the 150 years since Darwin's time, the 19th century argument against a creation event was completely debunked. The foundation for assuming the absence of a Creator completely evaporated in the face of 20th century science. Today, evolution can be viewed as a mechanism for supporting biological diversity, but it says absolutely nothing about the origin of life. Although Richard Dawkins is one of the world's most vocal atheists, the field of science from which he draws his arguments (evolutionary biology) has proven to be not relevant to the question of whether God is real or not.

Richard Dawkins acknowledges that evolution does not yet address mechanisms for the origin of life but he continues to believe that science will someday fill in the unknown details. For this, after 150 years, he has no evidence. Examined closely, rationally, logically, Dawkins's position can be seen to include no fact that resolves the God / No God dichotomy. Dawkin's messages regarding God are not based upon relevant science. They are nothing but declarations of faith, his personal anti-faith. This atheist rejects God and urges others to reject God based upon nothing stronger than his personal set of beliefs. He is demonstrably wrong.

In his book, _The God Delusion_, Dawkins summarizes his view of the progression of carbon-based life from less-complex through more-complex forms. He claims that mind takes form through a mindless reorganization of matter. As material organization becomes more complex, the expression of mind emerges from mindlessness. Central to his view is the expectation that matter comes first and mind comes next. The more complex the mind, the more complex the required material structure.

To the atheist, matter is the primary construct of life. Mind is a secondary product of matter. To those of faith, matter is a secondary construct of this cosmos. That distinction is central to sorting out the resolution of whether God is possible, plausible, proven, or ruled out.

Dawkins argues that the complexity of this world can be explained **only** by progressive change from simple to complex. The atheist's assertion requires that the correlation is always demonstrated as matter before mind. More complex material organization is the prerequisite for more complex mindfulness. That strict correlation between material complexity and the complexity of mind is critical to determining whether the atheist assertion has merit. We will find that it does not have merit. Mindfulness demonstrated through correct ancient teaching of the true cosmic structure before that structure could be physically measured breaks Dawkins's required correlation.

Dawkins challenges that any argument favoring the existence of God must start with an explanation for how God came to exist in the first place. In order to consider the possibility that God caused this world, Dawkins demands an explanation for what caused God. One might argue that Dawkins's demand is unreasonable, but in this book I will accept his challenge and turn it back on him. We will examine the facts that establish why it is scientifically reasonable to accept God as a primary cause without need for any prior cause. We will then examine the modern facts that prove that matter is not the primary construct of this universe. We will see that matter is a secondary by-product of a more primary entity, energy. We will then examine facts that establish a reason for concluding that mindfulness can and does exist independently of matter. The evidence for that mind will be documentation of the capacity to communicate in a way that demonstrates factual knowledge beyond that of humanity. This is knowledge held before mankind had the capacity to physically measure that which was known. We will demonstrate that the facts known by this immaterial mind include details that simply were not known to the bronze-age humans who first recorded these truths of nature. Any logical and reasonable analyst will be forced to acknowledge that this information argues for the rejection of the atheistic hypothesis that there is no God. Instead, this information argues strongly in favor of the reality of God as introduced to humanity through Genesis Chapter 1.

Let us address the challenge that a cause for God must be identified in scientific terms. To Dawkins, I respond that:

"Energy is; therefore, God could be."

What this statement means is that God, like energy, needs no further cause. God is adequately self-defined, just as is the case for energy.

Physics recognizes that energy is absolutely real, while being explained only as 'the capacity for action.' Fundamental concepts like force, work, and power are defined using the unchallenged recognition that energy simply is. Energy is accepted as a primary cause without need of a prior cause. I claim that the existence of an immaterial God meeting all fundamental characteristics of energy needs no explanation beyond that demanded by science for energy.

God is immaterial. Like energy, God is without beginning or end. God is the ultimate capacity to act. He has acted and He remains active.

Modern science recognizes the undisputed presence of a universal pool of energy. This energy is transformable and interchangeable but incapable of being created or destroyed. This universal force is indivisible but is simultaneously active on a scale as small as that of subatomic physics and as large as that of interstellar physics. This force is universally active in the mediation of physical phenomena such as the laws of mass action that underlie the chemical and physical functions for all living cells. It is impossible to study science and not appreciate the multiple demonstrations of intelligence associated with the actions of this universal force. It is scientifically unjustified to witness the activities of this universal force and not acknowledge the possibility that this underlying, universal, force is a reflection of God.

"Energy is, therefore God could be" might be misinterpreted as a version of the pagan belief of pantheism. Pantheism simply defines a god or collection of gods as the totality of the physical universe around us. What I describe is not pantheism. Pantheism is pagan in that it does not extend to God the full status of a living being, indeed the supreme living being. God is not simply the amalgamation of all that is. God is the prime cause of all that is.

"Energy is, therefore God could be" should not be misinterpreted to mean that God is the simple equivalent of physical energy, directly measured when we measure energy. Although the faithful recognize God's real presence manifested through His creation, we also believe that the scope of God is scaled on a level grander than the simple aggregation of inanimate energy. The energy that we measure is constrained to the four dimensions of our spacetime. God is not constrained within these four dimensions of spacetime. Electricity is not alive. God is alive.

'Energy is, therefore God could be' is a statement fully consistent with modern science. As such, God deserves at least a basic presumption as a scientific possibility. We can extend this further. As the 20th century progressed, one finding after another consistently added to a body of evidence supporting the conclusion that God is **scientifically plausible**. The declaration that faith is supported by no evidence is false. Today, the argument of the atheist is completely devoid of scientific support. The portrayal of atheism as a conclusion driven by modern science is nothing but bluster. It is false and misleading bluster.

The Defense of Faith – The Argument in a Nutshell

In his atheistic argument, _God, The Failed Hypothesis_, Victor Stenger demonstrates multiple blatant examples of a 'straw dog argument,' an argument waged against a false restatement of the position of the debate opponent.[13] Stenger starts any number of arguments with a description of God structured as noun with adjective, like 'a perfectly loving God.' He would then describe facts of life in this world such as, 'innocent babies die.' He then sweeps in with linguistic editorial declaring that the death of innocent babies is not a demonstration of perfect love, "...therefore there is no God." This trick of arguing against God through linguistic attacks against theological adjectives is not unique to Stenger, but he was one of the best at making the argument sound unbeatable. It is not.

It is important to realize that the existence of God does not rest upon whether or not one can argue against the adjectives applied by theologians to expand and extend human understanding of God. The atheist cannot argue against God by attacking the 4th century writings of Augustine. The argument against God must be structured against the essential existence of God as described by God. The Bible starting with Genesis Chapter 1, is that description of God by God.

---

[13] Stenger, Victor J. God: The Failed Hypothesis. How Science Shows That God Does Not Exist. Amherst, NY., Prometheus Books, 2007 ISBN 9 781591024811

Stenger is featured at this point of the book not merely to describe the fallacies of his argument techniques. Stenger is featured here because he vocalized challenges against faith in ways that help establish a scientific basis for contrasting atheism versus faith. This contrast will disprove the validity of atheism. This scientific contrast won't resolve in detail whether it is better to worship as a Jew or a Christian, but it will establish the credibility of God as revealed through the opening chapter of these ancient Hebrew Scriptures. (In the final chapter, I will discuss how I personally resolve this question. I am Christian but I fully understand and respect the faithful choices of those who carry forward a never-ending fidelity to Judaism.)

Stenger acknowledged that even the most strident of skeptics could be made to reconsider if the faithful could present even one strong piece of factual evidence in support of God. He claims that this could never be done, and explicitly argues that the Bible has been proven to be factually wrong. His dismissal of the Bible actually establishes the basis for refutation of his position. Stenger contrasts the known facts of the origin of our universe against his understanding of the biblical description of the origin. He points out that the Bible is wrong with respect to the following points:

1) Age of the universe: The universe is older than the age derived from the human genealogies of the Bible.
2) Duration of the creation sequence: The process for formation and maturation of our universe took longer than six consecutive earth-days.
3) Order of creation of Earth, then Light, then Sun and Moon: He says the Bible claims that Earth was created on day 1 with the sun on day 4.

Stenger claims that if the Bible cannot even get these early facts right, then nothing in the Bible can be believed. Thank you, Dr. Stenger, for perfectly staging the scientific contrast between atheism and faith. As with other straw dog arguments, Stenger's paraphrase of what the Bible says is wrong, rendering his arguments completely wrong. What we will find is that science completely supports the text of Genesis Chapter 1. Using the corollary of Stenger's argument, if

Genesis Chapter 1 is fully credible, then the balance of the Bible has earned credibility as well.

Stenger rejects any evidence drawn from Biblical prophesy because humans could have falsified reality through intentional self-fulfillment. What Stenger demanded of the Scriptures is the inclusion of a "dangerous prediction." This would be a prediction of something not likely to occur by chance and which could not possibly be fulfilled through intentional self-fulfillment. He was looking for an ancient prediction of something that could not have possibly been known at the time of the first recording. He demanded prophesy as dramatic as the foretelling that mankind will someday travel to the moon and demonstrate reduced gravity by driving a golf ball beyond the reach of human vision.

Today, we find that a comparison of the Genesis scriptures against modern science perfectly satisfies Stenger's demands. Let me repeat that. The Genesis Chapter 1 scriptures satisfy the demand for the fulfillment of dangerous prophesy. The author of Genesis Chapter 1 knew details that pre-scientific humans working alone simply would not know. The author of Genesis 1 knew details that even modern humans could not know until well into the 20th century.

"Energy is, therefore God could be" is a statement reflecting the fact that **God is scientifically possible**. Following Stenger's challenge, the faithful can present an even bolder statement. Not only is God scientifically possible, but **God is scientifically plausible.** Not less than three biblical declarations have been tested and they have tested well.

1. This world did have a beginning
2. This world is the result of something made from nothing.
3. The first step was the emergence of light.

Ancient man could not have invented a story with these details. Not even 19th century man could have made these assertions. The science of the 20th century provided the first evidence supporting scientific understanding of the mechanisms through which this universe began. It turns out that the details of those ancient scriptures are truly prescient. The scriptural phrase, "Let there be light," is not merely symbolic. The emergence of light was literally the first step of creation. That detail could not have been the invention of ancient humans. Furthermore, mainstream science has not been researched and reported by humans intent on self-fulfillment of the scriptures. To any reviewer willing to judge fairly, the modern confirmation of the details of Genesis Chapter 1 has earned a strong measure of credibility for the Bible.

Einstein earned respect for his Theory of Relativity because his advance predictions have been verified. Among other details, Einstein predicted that gravity would bend the path of a light beam because it would actually bend the space through which light traveled. Upon first prediction, this could not be tested. However, Einstein's predictions became testable and his advance predictions have been confirmed. Similar merit has been earned by the advance predictions laid out in Genesis Chapter 1.

Modern science confirms the scriptural record. This world did have a beginning. That beginning required the emergence of something made from nothing. Light was the first step in that beginning. Space, time, and matter (firmament) simultaneously came into existence as the second step. The mechanism for this was the transformation of light into matter according to $e=mc^2$. Within space, the stars and systems of stars then took form. After the formation of stars, the Sun-Earth-Moon system was formed. Life emerged in the order presented in the scriptures. Plant life preceded animal life. Animal life in the sea preceded animal life on land. Humans were the last of all animals to emerge. Just as confirmation of Einstein's prediction earned a measure of respect, so should the confirmation of these ancient biblical truths. Respect has not been received, but this is not the result of weakness of the facts supporting faith. It is a reflection of the fact that atheism stubbornly persists despite the facts, not because of the facts of science.

The continued aggression of atheism in the face of modern facts demonstrates that atheism is driven by a motivation other than pursuit of truth. The truth is that the arguments of the modern atheist are like those of a desperate court house lawyer. The atheists will twist any fact as needed to support their bias against God.

Atheists expect that most people will not drill down on the details. In this book, we will not give atheism a pass. We will drill down on the details. In the closing paragraphs of this chapter, let me illustrate some key examples that reflect distortion of truth by those who oppose God. In the chapters that follow we will closely examine the foundation of 20th century science relating to the plausibility of our Creator. With that detail in hand, we will return for a fact-based dissection of the atheist argument. We will find that the atheist argument is soundly refuted by modern science. Atheism is based upon a great big lie, a continuation of the most ancient of all lies.

The atheist, Richard Dawkins, regularly participates in public debates against those of faith. Those debating in support of faith have recently introduced the argument that the 20th century confirmation of a universal beginning is evidence in support of faith in God. Dawkins has introduced a unique but patently false tactic for debating against this claim. Dawkins now argues that the distinction between a universe with a beginning versus one without a beginning is simply a trivial point that never had any relevance to the argument of whether God was real or not. He describes the beginning of this universe as simply a 50:50 proposition with no relevance to the debate between atheism and faith. When Dawkins argues that a universe with a beginning is nothing more than a trivial distraction, he misrepresents true history.

The truth is that the atheistic community did not consider this issue trivial before the 1970s. Before this issue was finally resolved in the

1960s and 1970s, atheistic leadership argued strongly against any notion of a universe with a beginning. Recall that there has only been one scientific argument directly antagonistic to the possibility of a Creator. The 19th century atheistic scientists were certain that the universe could not possibly have been created because matter could not be created. Einstein's early work reversed that error but did not convert him from atheism. Einstein actually 'fudged' an artificial adjustment into his work to support his bias that the universe had existed eternally, with no beginning. (Einstein later described that adjustment as the greatest blunder of his life). Fred Hoyle and other atheists of the early- and mid-20th century argued strongly in favor of the steady state (always existing) model of the universe. The literal term, "Big Bang" was coined by Fred Hoyle as an attempt to demean the emerging new model which he recognized as a threat to the atheist worldview. Stephen Hawking developed mathematical models of black holes in the 1970s that provided the mathematical confirmation for the beginning of the universe. He then spent the balance of his active career searching for a revision that could continue to support the atheist arguments against a creation event. He failed in that endeavor.

The truth is that the argument of the atheistic scientist through the 19th and most of the 20th century was that this universe did not have a beginning. Dawkins misleads when he claims that this issue has no relevance to the consideration of the reality of God. This issue is big and he should know it. The fact that this world did, indeed, have a beginning is bad news for the atheistic worldview.

Atheistic scientists like Victor Stenger argue that the ancient Genesis scriptures have been proven false, but they specifically attack straw dog arguments. Stenger specifically argues against only the overly literalistic interpretation held by the minority of all faithful. Stenger argues that the Bible is false because the origin of this universe took longer than six days. Stenger and others mislead by staging arguments against a false presentation of what those scriptures actually portray. In doing so, atheists work to prevent generalized recognition of the strong match between modern science and the day-age interpretation of scripture. In arguing against a false premise, Stenger obscures truth but cannot erase it.

As we progress through this book, we will find support for the truth, the whole truth. In doing so, however, I am sorry to say that my arguments will simultaneously be subjected to challenge from two quite different viewpoints. To support the whole truth, I must argue not only against the atheist, but also against those who insist on the incorrect interpretation of Genesis as a short period of six consecutive earth-days. That interpretation of scripture is wrong scientifically and it is wrong theologically. That error is harmful to the defense of faith. That error paradoxically hides the full glory of God's brilliant work. The truth is that Genesis Chapter 1 reflects a literally true description of God's creative work. However the literal truth of Genesis can only be recognized when you avoid taking the wrong word literally.

It is impossible to ignore the irony that today's overly literalistic interpretation of scripture is just like that medieval error of the Roman Catholic Church. Today, the issue is not a question of the orbit of the earth around the sun but is the definition of a scriptural 'day.' That issue is exactly reflective of those who opposed Galileo. The truth is that the earth does orbit around the sun. That overly literalistic interpretation of the medieval Church proved to be wrong. The truth also includes the fact that God's creative process spanned more than six consecutive earth-days. We all need to embrace the life lesson that this fact teaches.

The whole truth is that science is completely aligned with the expectation that our universe was created by God according to the six sequential steps laid out in the scriptures of the ancient Hebrews. This process was sequential as described in Genesis, but was not short. However, atheists such as David Silverman, argue that it is not valid for those of faith to 'change' our interpretation of the meaning of scripture to improve the match against the facts of science. Silverman argues that the debate between science and religion must be constructed according to historical interpretations of scripture.[14] He specifically attacks a variety of topics such as 6-day creation sequence, use of clay to form Adam, emergence of Earth before the emergence of Earth's sun, and other overly literalistic interpretations of scripture. In his argument, Silverman insists that the faithful must adhere to the most literal of all interpretations. He is wrong.

Atheists do not get to define how scripture is to be interpreted. They do not get to falsely stage straw dog arguments targeting inaccurate summaries of the scriptures. Truth is the highest pursuit of both science and religion, and the atheist does not get to distort the conditions for that pursuit.

In this book we will establish reasons to understand that the Bible starts with a telling of absolute truth – scientifically confirmed truth. The Bible does not start with truth only to fail miserably thereafter. The Bible continues as a fully trustworthy record of the communication between God and humanity. However, it is critical that these scriptures be studied and understood correctly. Overly literalistic interpretation ignores the complex divine messaging behind these scriptures. These scriptures address the needs for teaching humanity throughout all stages of human development. It is false to read these scriptures only through the eyes of modern humanity. These scriptures have been structured to guide generations of simple humans who would never know about the machines and concepts of modernity. The scriptures are much broader and deeper than that reflected in overly literalistic interpretation. Let me illustrate.

---

[14] Silverman, David. Fighting God; An Atheist Manifesto For a Religious World New York, Thomas Dunne Books, St. Martin's Press, 2015 ISBN. 9781250064844

Atheists like Silverman challenge as absurd the idea that the human body was formed by the infusion of life into a hunk of clay. It is true that ancient scriptures say that God formed the first human male by breathing the human soul into clay but ridicule of this scripture is another instance of the atheist setting up a straw dog argument. It is important to realize that the majority of faithful do not follow a mandate of interpretation of this scripture as reflective of a literal sculpting of the first human body, including every capillary and neuron, from potter's clay. It is fully valid to interpret these scriptures as God's revelation that He formed male and female humans from preexisting organic biomaterial (aka, clay). The faithful understand that we have been made from dust and will return to dust. This is also true of all other animals, so divine use of a living primate as the incubator for the first human soul does not present a conflict between scripture and science.

It is important to look at the details of the Creation of man. For those who hold strongly to the 6-day creation duration I ask you to think about the reason God created man starting with clay, or any preexisting material. Why did he not simply cause humanity to appear as some believe he ordered for the primordial planet, Earth. The scriptures reveal that God works through His own mechanisms. The only thing that came from nothing was light. For everything else, God used a precursor. THINK about what that teaches.

The story of Noah is the next teaching lesson (as it is the next greatest source of conflict between some of faith and those of science). I do not hold a literal belief that Noah saved *the ancestors of every modern animal species* using a single boat built of wood. However, I believe that the scriptural story of Noah reflects knowledge of the modern understanding of an event of near-extinction for all human life. The human genetic record demonstrates a restriction of DNA variability consistent with the demise of all but a small band of Homo sapiens. This band of survivors was small enough to reflect the genetic tree of as few as 2000 total humans (combination of actual survivors and genetic ancestors of those survivors.) All modern human life has descended from that very small group of survivors and this is consistent with the story of Noah. This story reflects ancient reality, true human history, whether or not every single species of modern animal life was taken aboard a single boat.

As we progress through this book, we will establish the basis for trusting that the Bible is truthful and without error when those scriptures are interpreted in view of the full cosmic scope of God. While the Bible is absolutely true, the Galileo affair demonstrates that mankind does not always understand the full cosmic scope of God. We can err. We can misinterpret details. We can fail to differentiate between those details that are literal versus those statements that are allegorical. As we approach the end of this book we will address the issue of why God is both real and not easy to understand. For now, suffice to demonstrate that human error is real and this human error extends to the interpretation of scripture.

However, human error with respect to scriptural interpretation does not represent a weakness of the scriptures. Indeed, in these very mature days of human history, documented human error actually provides a mechanism for establishing that the match between scripture and modern science is not the product of human self-fulfillment. Human error with respect to these scriptures actually helps isolate that which comes from mankind from that which originates from beyond mankind. These scriptures are not the invention of mankind. These scriptures originate from a mind beyond that of ancient humanity.

Genesis starts with the declaration, "IN THE BEGINNING God created the heavens and earth", and some misinterpret this to mean that planet Earth came into existence through instantaneous apparition at the first step. Atheists love to argue against this proposition because the facts show that planet Earth was a late arrival. As with the 6-day interpretation of the duration of the creation sequence, the idea that planet Earth was formed on the first day is incorrect linguistically, theologically, and scientifically. This error need not be permanent.

Genesis Chapter 1 opens as follows:

1 In the beginning, [when] God created the heavens and the earth
2 and the earth was without form or shape, with darkness over the abyss and a mighty wind sweeping over the waters—
3 Then God said: Let there be light, and there was light.
4 God saw that the light was good. God then separated the light from the darkness.
5 God called the light "day," and the darkness he called "night." Evening came, and morning followed—the first day.

Since the 1950s, the Roman Catholic Church has taught that the first two verses of Genesis Chapter 1 do not reflect activity linked specifically to the first step of the creation sequence.[15] It is linguistically correct to interpret the first two verses as an introduction to that which follows, an executive summary, if you will. That introduction prepares the reader to understand that there was a beginning, God was the Creator, His starting point was a void (held nothing) and that which follows explains how this creation was brought about. The first divine act of creation was the bringing forth of light; "Let there be light." Attention to light was not simply the act of God turning on a task light over His work table. This tells us how God initiated creation.

Let us closely examine the sequence of Genesis Chapter 1 and see how that matches step-by-step with the scientific understanding of the origin of our universe. The biblical record is paraphrased first (left,

---

[15] Footnote from http://www.usccb.org/bible/genesis/1 "This section, from the Priestly source, functions as an introduction, as ancient stories of the origin of the world (cosmogonies) often did. It introduces the primordial story…Until modern times the first line was always translated, "In the beginning God created the heavens and the earth." Several comparable ancient cosmogonies, discovered in recent times, have a "when…then" construction, confirming the translation "when…then" here as well. "When" introduces the pre-creation state and "then" introduces the creative act affecting that state. The traditional translation, "In the beginning," does not reflect the Hebrew syntax of the clause."

no indentation, **bold font**) followed by the scientific record (indented, not bolded, *italic font*)

Executive Summary of Genesis Chapter 1

IN THE BEGINNING... God created the heavens and earth. The starting point was the absence of anything. This is an introductory statement applicable to all steps that follow. This is not a description of the first step per se.

> *There was indeed a beginning; this universe has not existed forever. The starting point held no matter, no time, and no space. Planet Earth was not formed as a first step; Earth was a late addition to the universe.*

The First Day (Age)

"Let there be Light" was the first creative step.

> *Light, intensely hot electromagnetic radiation (EMR), was the first step of the origin of the universe.*

The Second Day (Age)

After the creation of light and before the emergence of life of any type, firmament (the sky), was formed. As per Psalms 104, the heavens were spread out like a tent. Into the firmament the lights of the sky were placed.

> *The scaffolding of space burst into existence from no prior space like the opening of a parachute. Precipitation of matter from pure energy according to $e=mc^2$ directly caused this. Stars formed as the earliest and still predominant structures in space.*

The Emergence of Life, on Multiple Days (Ages) 3, 5 and 6

The emergence of life proceeded with plant life first and humans last. Animal life in the sea preceded animal life on land. Plant life originated on 'Day 3', animal life on 'Day 5' and Humans on 'Day 6'.

The known pattern of the emergence of life matches the ancient declaration that plants preceded animals and sea animals preceded land animals. Humans were last.

The Fourth Day (Age)

Between the emergence of plant life and the emergence of animal life, additional attention is directed to Earth and its two great lights yielding a time–compliant system, marking the passage of seasons, days and years.

The Sun-Earth-Moon system was a late addition to the universe. The final adjustment and control of the earth's rotational axis by the moon completed a finely tuned clockwork mechanism that optimally distributes seasonality across the earth.

The Sixth Step – The Dawn of Humanity

Humans were the last of all animals to be created and differed from all other animals through the unique gift of a soul / mind that was created as an image of God. The human soul / mind is a reflection of the creative, thinking Being who conceived and constructed this universe.

Humans demonstrated the most recent emergence of any species of animal. Nodal branching of the higher branches of the 'tree of life' has not continued after the emergence of the human. No other animal rivals the creative drive and capacity of the human mind.

The match between the scriptural and scientific record of the formation of our universe is complete. The change from nothing into something began with light as the first step. The second step involved the creation of space where space had not previously existed. The formation of stars followed the formation of space. The emergence of life proceeded with plant life first and humans last. Animal life in the sea preceded animal life on land. Between the emergence of plant life and the emergence of marine life, additional attention appears directed to the orientation of the Sun-Earth-Moon system. Humans were the last of all animals to be created and would differ from all other animals through the unique gift of God-like soul/ mind.

With respect to the sequence of the origin of life, the match between Genesis and the best current understanding of the relative order of the emergence of life is absolutely astounding. The idea that life originated as plant life, before completion of the moon, is incredibly well matched to modern scientific concepts that conditions for first life might have been quite different from those required for the stable progression toward more advanced forms of life. This even remains consistent with the possibility that primordial life originated beyond the confines of Earth, with transference via interstellar collision.

It is absolutely correct to review these ancient scriptures according to the day-age interpretation. When this is done, we find that Genesis Chapter 1 is fully concordant with the modern measurements of this world. The truth is that faith in the Bible is not in conflict with science when we understand how to read scripture from a perspective of God's totality, not simply from the perspective of Earthlings. I invite you to explore the details in the balance of the chapters of this book.

The next two chapters will provide an introduction to the foundations of relativity theory. First we will explore the details of the relativistic effect called time dilation. With that background, a full understanding of that famous equation, $e=mc^2$, is brought within our reach. In the process, we will cover mathematical details that are typically omitted from popular summaries of science.

As I studied works describing science for the popular market, I found that math was completely avoided. It was both the implied and explicit declaration of the authors that the relevant math was too tedious for any except those fully trained in advanced science.

Absent the fundamental math, I found that the pursuit of truth involved an endless review of one book after another taking the form of a battle of words against words. The faithful defended faith. The atheists attacked faith. It all became a matter of semantics and word twists. I remained helplessly dependent upon the editorial bias of the author. What I needed was something that would help me sort out bedrock from simple rhetoric. Digging into the math proved helpful.

Only upon direct study of Einstein's personal attempt to describe relativity theory for the general reader did I find my first exposure to the critical equation called the Lorentz-Fitzgerald equation. This equation takes less than one square inch on a printed page but reveals scientific fact so rich that full library sections are needed to describe those facts with words. That is why we should not avoid the basic math.

The Lorentz-Fitzgerald equations describe the interconnected behaviors of light, matter and space. Even though this equation represents the foundation for some of the most advanced of all 20th century science, it can be understood by all of us. Full understanding can be achieved using nothing more complex than 9th grade multiplication, division, and subtraction, with one very powerful square root determination.

If you bear with me through this text, you will read that Einstein concluded that the speed of light is the fastest possible speed in this universe. If you follow the math, you will understand exactly why Einstein came to that conclusion. From that starting point, using a step-by- step process similar to work done in 7th through 9th grades, you can follow a simple derivation of Einstein's most famous equation, $e = mc^2$. From this foundation, you will gain the opportunity to examine the role of light as the first step in the process of universal creation. This will set the stage for truly understanding things that might seem like science fiction if described using nothing other than words.

Supported by this mathematical foundation, you will enjoy the capacity to reflect on concepts like timelessness and omnipresence. In the past these concepts would seem purely theological, but they are scientifically meaningful today. We will see that time, space, and mass are all dependent upon the relative speed of travel. These apparently bedrock features of our world are actually not a permanent feature of reality but are as malleable as potter's clay. Indeed, in the immaterial realm of pure energy, the concepts of time, space, and mass are truly undefined, like a division by zero. For thousands of years, God has been said to be timeless. With 20th century science, this concept takes on true physical meaning. God is said to be omnipresent, meaning everywhere at once. This is scientifically practical when distance becomes meaningless. For pure energy, distance is meaningless.

We are going to come to understand the details of how matter could have come from no prior matter. To understand that, we must understand Einstein's equation, $e=mc^2$. No matter how many times I looked at this equation, I never understood what it meant until I understood how Einstein came up with it in the first place. This is why we will work through the math. If you find it difficult, try your best. Reflect for a while. Ask another person for help. Try to make your way through this math. If needed, continue onward through the narrative and try to go back a time or two. You may find that the math clears up after you move through some of the implications of that math as explained in text. For those who do trudge through this work, you will find an understanding of nature that protects you from being dismissed as ignorant by an atheist who speaks with the illusion of intelligence but without true knowledge.

Before tackling the next two chapters, let me share one tip that I have learned through my personal experiences with math. Many times, my problem was not the inability to execute the individual steps of the math. What my real problem often boiled down to was difficulty recognizing why the rearrangement steps were taken in the order that they were presented. How did the teacher know in advance that a particular step should be taken at that particular point in the problem? What experience taught me was that a problem can be solved in a lot of different ways, sometimes with a requirement to go back to an earlier form and take a different tactic. With the math that follows, we want to avoid the trap of trying to recreate the arduous task of the original discovery by Einstein. We are not trying to compete with the genius of Einstein; we are simply trying to follow what he did. The fact is that hundreds of scientists had the same information that Einstein did, but none thought to do what he did. We do not need to rival Einstein's accomplishment as a trail blazer. We just need to follow the trail that he blazed. I assure you; we can do that.

Based upon an assessment that is deeper than a battle between my words and those of other authors, you will be able to form a personal assessment of truth. When you complete this book, you can accept or reject my assessment that God is completely consistent with modern science. Either way, your personal decision regarding faith will be based upon a very clear understanding of what science says and what it does not say. You will be prepared to make optimal use of your personal logic and reason.

I am confident that you will come to agree that science has not disproven God. You will see that science is fully supportive of faith in the God of the Bible. You will come to understand that atheistic authors who claim allegiance to logic and reason have not presented the full story. You will find that you do not have to choose between accepting science or faith. You will find that it is possible to embrace both science and faith. Truth does not conflict with truth. The presence of our Creator is clear for all to see in the truthful scientific measurements of this world.

Chapter 3. Time Is an Illusion

As early as the 4th century AD, St. Augustine wrote of time as something easily understood until the need arises to describe and explain it. Explaining time would not get much easier for centuries, and that is not to say that it is simple now.

Before reading further, take some time to think about your personal sense of time. Can you describe what time is? Is there an absolute time? Does one hour last the same duration in all places (i.e., in Chicago, on the moon, and on the surface of the sun)? If religious belief holds that God is not bound by time, but transcends time, is that concept scientifically feasible or is this a completely metaphysical concept?

My short answers to these questions are:

Can you describe what time is?

> Time is one of the four dimensions of spacetime in our physical universe, but it is not a primary construct. Time is a secondary feature defined by the behavior of mass. (See Appendix 2 for a definition of time as a rearrangement of Sir Isaac Newton's Equation, f=ma.)

Is there an absolute time?

> Unquestionably, there is no such thing as absolute time. Time is relative based upon the behavior of matter in any local area. Without matter, time isn't even defined.

Does one hour last the same duration in all places (e.g., in Chicago, on the moon, and on the surface of the sun?)

> The duration of one second will not be the same under the different gravitational forces experienced at the surfaces of the earth, the moon and the sun. Time is relative. The strength of local gravitational pull changes the relative value for a unit of time.

If religious belief holds that God is not bound by time, but exists in a realm that transcends time, is that concept scientifically feasible or is this a completely metaphysical concept?

> The concept of transcendence beyond time is fully consistent with modern science. For pure energy, time is meaningless.

In the 19th and 20th centuries the study of light, electricity and magnetism provided the foundations for the greatest advancements in physical science since the time of Sir Isaac Newton. One of those advancements was the theory of relativity as taught by Albert Einstein. A central feature of Einstein's theory of relativity is the finding that time is not an absolute feature of reality. Time is malleable. Time is relative.

Depending upon the relative behavior of mass, different places in space experience time under widely differing values for the duration of any 'tic' of the clock. For pure energy, a single 'tic' never comes to completion. Pure energy does not experience the passage of time. For pure energy, existence is timeless.

Time becomes a measurable quantity only in the presence of matter traveling slower than the speed of light. As physical creatures, our fastest speeds of travel are so slow that the passage of time appears to represent a regular, inescapable, bedrock feature of existence. However, this is an illusion caused by our very slow speeds of travel.

Time Dilation – The Lorentz-Fitzgerald Equation

The absence of any universal standard for the rate at which time passes is one of several counterintuitive details of Einstein's theory of relativity. The 'tic' of a clock takes longer to pass under some conditions than it does in others. Fast speed of travel or intense acceleration causes time to pass more slowly relative to the passage of time at rest. Einstein coined the term, "time dilation" to describe this slowing of time with fast relative motion.

Time dilation is imperceptible at speeds possible before the 20th century. However, when speed becomes very fast or gravity becomes very intense, time slows measurably. When travel velocity approaches the speed of light, the correction factor for the actual duration of each tic of the clock becomes huge relative to that for stationary objects. At the exact speed of light, time loses all meaning. Time becomes the result of division by zero.

A relatively simple equation called the Lorentz-Fitzgerald correction describes the elastic change in time based upon speed of travel. Popular descriptions of science almost never mention the existence of this equation, and never discuss it in mathematical detail. However, the Lorentz-Fitzgerald correction is critical to deeper understanding of Einstein's relativity theory, and it is within the reach of the non-scientist. We will explore this equation mathematically as well as through words. This effort on the part of the reader will support a truly deep and rich understanding of some of the most amazing features of the world around us.

First, it is important to know that time dilation is not simply a theoretical possibility. Time dilation has been confirmed through more than one practical demonstration. Today, the most commonly experienced real-world demonstration of time dilation is its incorporation into the engineering of modern GPS navigation systems. Relative to a car on Earth's surface, the GPS satellites experience significant differences in relative speed and gravitational pull. Without precise correction for the time dilation caused by these differences in speed and gravity, your electronic navigation unit simply would not work.

GPS navigation units work by determining the distances between the GPS unit and at least three orbiting satellites. By accurately measuring these distances, a single location on the map of Earth's surface can be calculated using mathematical triangulation (we won't dive into those details). Distance is measured by "pinging" electromagnetic signals from the GPS satellites to GPS receivers on earth. Those signals declare the time on the highly accurate clock on the satellite. This time is compared to a standard clock time on Earth. The time elapsed between satellite transmission and ground-based reception measures the distance of separation. These distances are used to calculate the triangulated determination of location for your specific GPS. A mind-bending fact of relativity theory is that both the slow moving car and the fast moving satellite experience the approach of electromagnetic signal beams at exactly the same speed of light (about 300,000 Km per second), but they experience completely different definitions for the duration of each second.

The atomic clocks in the satellites experience time differently while traveling about 15,000 Km per hour faster than the slow moving GPS units on earth. At that relative speed, time marches forward about 7 nanoseconds per earth-day slower than experienced by an equally accurate clock held in a stationary position on earth. Differences in gravity provide a second source of potential calculation error. The atomic clocks held on earth experience a much stronger gravitational pull than the satellites orbiting about 20,000 Km above the earth's surface. Because of this difference in relative gravitational force, clocks on earth experience time about 45 nanoseconds per earth-day slower than clocks in the satellites. The programmed calculations for the global positioning satellite system must incorporate a net adjustment of about 38 nanoseconds per earth-day (45 – 7 = 38) to account for time dilation. Absent that correction, the GPS navigation system would incorrectly calculate distances leading to incorrect calculation of the location of the GPS unit upon a map. This real world engineering achievement proves that time dilation is absolutely true.

In the paragraphs above, I have specified the amount of time dilation per earth-day because the equations for time dilation would yield a different result if calculated for the relatively different gravitational fields of Earth's moon or other planets, like Mars. Scientific truth includes the fact that time is not a constant beat from a single drummer's drum. Local time changes as relative conditions change.

Time as Known to Isaac Newton

Before Einstein, time was considered a fundamental, unchanging, bedrock feature of our universe. Sir Isaac Newton developed mathematical equations that predict the movement of matter upon the application of force. In each of his basic definitions of classic physics, Newton incorporated an invariant unit of time.

One example of Newton's work is the equation that describes the acceleration of matter by force as a relationship between three variables:

1. The amount of material being moved
2. The force exerted against the object
3. The rate at which the object is accelerated.

$$Force = Mass * Acceleration \qquad \text{(Equation 1)}$$

As with every equation, Equation 1 can be rearranged and that arrangement allows us to focus on acceleration as the result (i.e., the left side of the equation).

$$Acceleration = \frac{Force}{Mass} \qquad \text{(Equation 2)}$$

What this relationship shows is intuitive to anyone who has ever struggled to move a load by personal physical exertion:

1) More massive things are harder to accelerate than less massive things.
2) More force accelerates any object faster than less force.

In Newton's equations, a factor called 'time' simply appears as though it is a fully understood universal feature without need of definition or qualification. Speed is defined as the 'distance traveled per unit of time'. Acceleration is defined as the 'amount of change in speed over a unit of time.' Newton was highly aware that forces could vary and the size of objects could vary, but he never imagined that the unit of time might vary as well. In all of Newton's work, the fundamental concept of time always appears as though the duration of one second is unquestionably understood and universally standardized.

Clocks ran at different 'times' routinely in the days of Newton, but this was always interpreted as the imperfect function of the clockworks. Control over the power sources that drove a clock, consistent reproduction of the working parts of the clock, and precise control over friction and other losses of energy were seen as the methods by which clocks could be perfected to show the constant progression of time. The idea that the local details of our material world actually played some role in defining the value of time, leading to multiple locally applicable durations of time, was never considered until Einstein rocked our world with his theory of relativity.

The Seeds of Relativity Theory

Newton's physics help establish the basis for prediction and measurement of the relative speeds and momentum for objects sent traveling between a physical sender and a physical receiver. The apparent speed of an object thrown between a sender and a receiver is a mathematical function that involves the speed and direction of the sender, the speed and direction of the receiver, and the speed and direction of the launch of the transferred object. These relationships break down when the transferred object is light, and that breakdown formed the basis for Einstein's theory of relativity. To understand that foundation for relativity, let us first review the basics of relative travel between physical objects.

Under Newtonian physics, the relative speed of travel of all material things is a summation of the launch speed of the transferred object plus the relative speeds of the sender and the receiver. Let us look at that one step at a time.

Assume that a boy can throw (launch) a rock at the speed of 15 miles per hour while sitting on a stationary bicycle. If he throws that rock from a bicycle traveling at 10 miles per hour, the rock will travel 25 miles per hour relative to the motionless ground.

$$15\ mph\ +\ 10\ mph\ =\ 25\ miles\ per\ hour$$

If that rock strikes the flat windshield of a car traveling the opposite direction at the rate of 25 miles per hour, the speed at which the two approach each other is the same as if a rock was propelled at 50 miles per hour toward a stationary object.

$$15mph\ +\ 10\ mph\ +\ 25\ mph\ =\ 50\ miles\ per\ hour$$

The windshield of that car experiences the rock at a relative speed of 50 miles per hour against its direction of travel. The motionless ground experiences the rock at a relative speed of 25 mph. The boy on the bicycle experiences the rock at a relative speed of only 15 mph. Clearly, the speed of travel of an object is completely **relative** to the frame of reference of the observer.

It is commonplace that moving objects can also see other moving objects as not moving at all. If the direction of the car in the above vignette is reversed to the same direction as the rock, then the relative speed of that rock is now zero miles per hour. The rock would appear motionless to a passenger in the car.

$$15mph\ +\ 10mph\ \textbf{minus}\ 25\ mph\ =\ 0\ miles\ per\ hour$$

This is experienced every time two cars travel in the same direction in adjacent lanes of a highway. Cars traveling in the same direction can be made to appear motionless, or slightly faster, or slightly slower relative to the other. Cars traveling in opposite directions will appear to be traveling at much faster speed than either car alone. The speed of any object has meaning only when considered relative to some other specific frame of reference. Speed of travel is relative.

Relative motion is true with respect to physical objects, but by the late 19th century, scientists were aware that relative speed calculations did not apply when the transfer between sender and receiver involved light. Regardless of the speed of the sender or the receiver, the speed of light between two objects is always the same speed – never faster and never slower.

Key background facts regarding the speed of light were confirmed through multiple independent experiments throughout the 1800s. Modern experiments have introduced no significant revisions of the measured speed of light since that time. We know that light travels through a vacuum at approximately 300,000 Km / second or 675,000,000 miles per hour. That velocity is abbreviated as 'c' in Einstein's equation:

$$e = mc^2 \qquad \text{Einstein's Famous Equation}$$

Light travels at the speed of light. Electricity travels at the speed of light. Magnetic force travels at the speed of light. There simply is never any variance in the transmission velocity of pure energy. Light transmitted from an object in space toward Earth approaches the earth at exactly the speed of light regardless of whether Earth is moving toward or away from the source of light. Regardless of the relative motion of the sender or the receiver, light always closes the gap at exactly the same measurable speed, the speed of light. [16]

As the 19th century ended, it was clear that the speed of light was completely invariant regardless of the relative travel of the sender and the receiver. Although one physical object can travel at a speed sufficient to make another physical object appear motionless, it is impossible to travel alongside a beam of light in such a way as to cause the light to appear motionless. In fact, light in a vacuum will never appear to travel even slightly slower. Light always travels at

---

[16] The rate of transmission of light is always the speed of light when the sender and receiver are objects of significant mass. This is not the case when the two traveling objects are both of inconsequential mass, such as subatomic particles propelled toward each other in an atom smasher. In an atom smasher, gap closure between two subatomic particles both traveling close to the speed of light approaches twice the speed of light.

exactly the speed of light, not more and not less, regardless of the relative speeds of the sender or the receiver.

The invariability of the speed of light was available for all to ponder by the late 1890s, but its deep meaning remained out of reach of all the leading scientists of that day. Albert Einstein, a young nobody, working at a nowhere job, became somebody when he published the first sophisticated and complete interpretation of all that this fact means.

Einstein considered the possibility that the invariance of the speed of light might mean that the factors defining speed must be changing instead. If the speed of light is invariant, then perhaps travel at high speeds causes a change in the underlying meaning of time and space. Einstein's insight was correct and the result of his work on this subject has forever changed our understanding of the world in which we live. **The speed of light is not relative, but the fundamental units of time and distance are!**

Only Einstein was adventurous enough to pursue the full implications of that concept, but the physical and mathematical foundations for this conclusion were already the products of science by the time Einstein was a college student. Others were aware of the basics, but only Einstein pulled it all together.

An Irish physicist, George Francis Fitzgerald (1838 – 1923), was the first to describe the mathematical ratio that is the foundation for key equations supporting Einstein's relativity theory. In 1893, Fitzgerald published his interpretation of experimental results that led him to conclude that the electron becomes shorter, squashed, in the direction of its travel. The change in length of the fast moving electron follows the multiple-step ratio presented in Equation 4.[17]

---

[17] Isaac Asimov, Volume II, Chapter 6, p 96, The Ether, **Understanding Physics**, Original ©1966, reprinted by Barnes and Noble Books, New York, 1993 ISBN 0880292512

$$\sqrt{1 - \frac{v^2}{c^2}} \quad \text{Equation 4}$$

Fitzgerald correctly predicted that speeds approaching light speed would change the actual values of length by a function of the ratio of actual speed (v) over the speed of light (c). The square of that ratio is subtracted from 1 and then the square root of that difference would define the proportion to which Fitzgerald expected electrons to be compressed. While mathematically correct, Fitzgerald's views regarding a change in electron length were not taken seriously until presented again in a different form five years later by the Dutch physicist Hendrik Lorentz.

Follow-up experiments focused primarily on changes in mass (which also follow the Fitzgerald ratio) because these changes are easier to measure than changes in the units of length on the scale of individual electrons. Although most of us might not have been in a position to design these experiments, they are simple enough that we can now understand how they worked and what they have taught us.

The relationship between mass and speed can be measured accurately as a function of an outward drift for any object rounding a corner at high speed. As any fan of NASCAR understands, faster cars drift to the outside of a rounded corner and this drift can be measured. The same is true of heavier cars. Outward drift is most extreme for cars that are both faster and heavier. That principle can be applied to studies of subatomic particles. The path of subatomic particles can be measured as paths etched into smoke clouds held between glass plates. The speed of the particle can be adjusted by controlling the amount of energy used to accelerate the particle. Corners or curves can be induced into the path of the subatomic particle by applying magnetic fields along the path of the particle. The sharpness of the curve can be controlled by adjusting the strength of those magnetic fields. This experimental technique could be used to measure the relative mass of various subatomic particles by measuring the relative amounts of outward drift in the traced curve of the particle for given conditions of energy input. These types of cloud chamber experiments started to show a pattern of exaggerated outward drift of particles propelled with higher and higher energies. When it became clear that these findings were not in error, that additional outward drift could only mean that the particles were getting heavier with the addition of new energy. The rate at which those particles became heavier followed a specific mathematical function. That function exactly matched the ratio first published by Fitzgerald.

With this type of work available as background, Einstein pulled together a complete picture. Energy was being transformed into mass. The relationship that describes this transformation matched that which also appeared to reflect shrinkage of length reported by Fitzgerald. If mass and length could be changed at speeds approaching the speed of light, then it is probable that time also is being changed at the speed of light. For Einstein, this would explain the invariable speed of light under all frames of reference. For Einstein the mystery of the unchanged speed of light could be explained if we assume that the relative velocity of travel changes the underlying units that make up the definition of speed (distance and time). **The measured speed of light does not change because the units of space and time change instead!** Travel close to the speed of light changes mass, and length, and time, according to Fitzgerald's ratio. Time dilates (increases in duration), length contracts (gets shorter in the direction of travel), and mass increases (in the same proportion as time dilation).

Although $e = mc^2$ is the most famous equation associated with relativity, the Lorentz-Fitzgerald equations are more fundamental. These equations describe the relative adjustments to length, time, and mass that led Einstein to his theory of relativity. Understanding those adjustments to length, time, and mass set the stage for understanding why $e = mc^2$.

The Lorentz-Fitzgerald Equations

The Lorentz-Fitzgerald equation for time dilation is given below. What this equation says is that true time (t') corrected for speed of travel, is a function of time as measured at rest (t), divided by Fitzgerald's ratio.

$$t' = f\left(\frac{t}{\sqrt{1-\frac{v^2}{c^2}}}\right) \text{ (Equation 5)}$$

Don't panic upon first reflection on this equation. It looks complicated, but it is just a collection of several steps and no single step is difficult. Table 1 shows the Lorentz-Fitzgerald equation worked out step-by-step for the two extreme situations of absolute rest and travel at the full speed of light. These equations yield mathematically simple results at these two extremes. After we understand these mathematically simple conditions, we can consider what happens at the intermediate conditions.

The left column of Table 1 shows a step-by-step calculation for corrected time when an object is at absolute rest and the right column shows the condition for the exact speed of light.

Before tackling these steps, let's review an important detail regarding division by zero because that is critical to understanding the right column of Table 1. If you divide any number by zero on your calculator, you get an error signal. That's not because division by zero breaks an arbitrary rule. Division by zero gives a result that is an undefined number, a value that has no place anywhere along a number line. When a calculation for a real-world thing requires a division by zero, it means that the real-world thing is undefined. It does not exist for that real-world condition. We will see that time does not exist when the speed of travel is the full speed of light in a vacuum.

Table 1 Lorentz-Fitzgerald Correction Step-By-Step	
When at rest, then $v = zero$	When actual speed equals the speed of light, then $v = c.$
Since v = zero, then $v^2 = zero$	Since v = c, then $v^2 = c^2.$
If $v^2 = zero,$ then $\frac{v^2}{c^2} = zero.$	If $v^2 = c^2,$ then $\frac{v^2}{c^2} = 1.$
If $\frac{v^2}{c^2} = 0,$ then $\left[1 - \left(\frac{v^2}{c^2}\right)\right] = 1,$ therefore $\sqrt{1 - \frac{v^2}{c^2}} = 1$	If $\frac{v^2}{c^2} = 1,$ then $\left[1 - \left(\frac{v^2}{c^2}\right)\right] = 0,$ therefore $\sqrt{1 - \frac{v^2}{c^2}} = 0$
$$t' = f\left(\frac{t}{1}\right)$$	$$t' = f\left(\frac{t}{0}\right)$$
t' is a function of t divided by 1 means that corrected time equals uncorrected time.	**t' is a function of t divided by 0** means that corrected **time is an undefined value.** For pure energy, time does not exist.
When at **rest**, corrected time (t') is not different relative to another object at rest (t)	When traveling at the **full speed of light,** corrected time (t') becomes undefined, the result of division by zero.
t = time as measured by object at rest; t'= corrected for travel speed	

These step-by-step calculations show that at rest, corrected time is unchanged. That is what Isaac Newton perceived. However, at the exact speed of light, the correction equation yields a value for corrected time that involves a division by zero. Division by zero yields an undefined number, so time is undefined at the speed of light. At the full speed of light, **timelessness is a true state of existence.**

Between these two extreme speeds (absolute rest versus speed of light), intermediate corrections are experienced. These intermediate corrections are graphed in Figure 1.

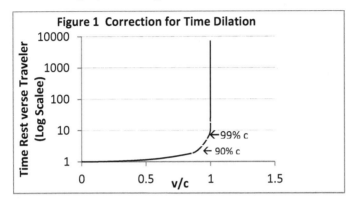

Figure 1 Correction for Time Dilation

In Figure 1, the horizontal axis is the ratio of actual speed divided by speed of light (v/c). The vertical axis shows the relative duration of corrected time compared to time at rest. The value of corrected time reflects the time passed by some object at rest compared to the passage of time experienced by the lapse of a single unit of time for a faster traveling object.

At speeds below 90% of the speed of light, the slope of this function is almost perfectly horizontal. That means that at speeds below about 270,000 Km per second, time dilation is so slight as to be imperceptible. Above 99% the speed of light, the change suddenly goes ballistic. Time dilation seems to shoot through the roof. At speeds very close to the speed of light, the duration of any unit of time is stretched out, dilated 100-fold or longer relative to the duration of time at rest.

At 90% of the speed of light, the object at rest ages about 2.3 seconds for every 1 second experienced by the traveler. At 99.0% of the speed of light, more than 7 seconds pass for every 1 second experience by the traveler. At 99.999999% the speed of light, almost 2 hours pass for every 1 second experience by the traveler. When travel speed exactly matches that of the speed of light, the mathematical correction for the value for a single unit of time takes on the mathematical value of division by zero.

Division by zero $\left(\frac{1}{zero}\right)$ in any physical condition is what physicists call a singularity. Physicists also speak of the mathematical value for division by zero as infinity. More properly, division by zero reflects the unique state of being mathematically undefined. Many people, including professional physicists, internalize incorrect concrete ideas of infinity. Even scientifically trained people mistakenly treat infinity as though it is a very large number, a number larger than any achievable number. This misperception causes many scientists, like Michio Kaku, to treat conditions involving division by zero as physical impossibilities. Kaku and others have publicly taught that conditions involving division by zero represent a boundary at which the laws of physics break down.

It is intimidating to teach opposite of minds such as Professor Kaku, but there is a better way to think about physical conditions involving division by zero. Division by zero, the state of infinity, is not an impossibly large number. It is an undefined number. Division by zero is a mathematical chasm, a complete void, with no place on any number line. For the physicist, division by zero should not suggest that the laws of physics have broken down. Division by zero simply means that the physical construct being studied is not defined under those conditions. Literally, when the actual value of time is corrected to a division by zero, this simply means that time is undefined under those physical conditions. For light traveling through a vacuum, time is undefined but that does not mean the laws of physics have broken down under those conditions.

So, What Does This Mean?

The Fitzgerald ratio takes less than 1 square inch of page space using the shorthand of mathematics but it reveals full chapters of information about our world. We will introduce key features now, and expand to reveal additional detail throughout the remaining chapters of this book.

The first thing that we should recognize is that a physical condition involving division by zero is not impossible and does not indicate a breakdown of the laws of physics. Light in a vacuum is a perfect teacher of the physical meaning of a division by zero. Light in a vacuum complies with all laws of physics while also being characterized by a division by zero for corrected values for time and mass. That means that details of this universe can be physically defined under some conditions but not physically defined under others. This is not impossible; this is scientific fact. That scientific fact reinforces ancient theological concepts. Scientific reinforcement of ancient theology should not remain hidden from public view.

Since antiquity, those who believe in the God of Abraham have held that God exists as a timeless Being. The concept of timelessness is not simply an abstract thought for theologians. Timelessness is a scientific reality. Timelessness is a real condition, descriptive of reality for pure energy.

Since antiquity, the faithful have believed in a beginning of time. This concept is not just theological poetry. Time did have a beginning. Before matter first formed, there would have been no time and no space. When matter first formed, time began.

Since antiquity, the faithful have believed that God is omnipresent, meaning present everywhere at once. This theological concept is scientifically meaningful. Under the conditions of undefined time, the value for the unit of distance is zero. When distance is zero, the idea of separation simply does not compute. When the unit of distance is zero, being every place is the same as being any place.

Next, we should fully appreciate the deep scientific and theological meaning of the fact that a single rule of nature simultaneously governs pure energy traveling at the speed of light and solid matter at complete rest. This single rule of mathematics applies without interruption at all speeds from absolute rest through the speed of light. An extreme j-hook in the mathematical behavior of this relationship brings about two completely different outward appearances, but matter and light are really of the same essence. Light and rock seem completely different, but they are expressions of the same entity, pure energy.

Matter, space and time are all byproducts of pure energy. We will see that space and time come into existence as secondary byproducts of the precipitation of matter from pure energy. Where there is no matter, there is no space and there is no time. When matter forms from conversion of pure energy, then the scaffolding of spacetime unfurls. Time and space take form and become defined as secondary features of the local behavior of matter.

Time is defined by the local behavior of matter. The broad range of correction factors for time dilation has profound implications for those who ponder the total universal age. The truth is that time is not the same in all places under all conditions. Think about this. **Time has not always been the same across all times.** As this universe took form from an initial structure of pure energy (therefore no matter, no space, and no time) until now, a complete spectrum of material structure and behavior took place.

This universe has progressed from
a) massless pure energy, to
b) almost-massless subatomic particles traveling at nearly the speed of light and distributed with nearly perfect homogeneity, to
c) the current state of mass densely clumped into gravitationally active stars and star systems separated by vast areas of empty space, along with
d) every intermediate stage between b and c above.

Through these changes, the complete range of various correction factors for time dilation applied for some relative fraction of the duration of all history. Correction factors ranging anywhere between

1 through more than 10,000 have been ignored by those who attempt to measure the age of very old things. This is not good news for those who confidently declare that the age of the universe is a full 13.77 billion years old. (To be discussed later, the facts are equally bad news for those who insist that the universe came into existence in only six consecutive 24-hour earth days.)

The most important thing for an enthusiast for any particular time frame to keep in mind is that time is meaningless unless you know the context of all relativistic corrections to be applied. Without detailed knowledge of the applicable correction factors, "time" is no better than "sea level" as a universally applicable standard of measurement. We will find that the basic unit of time has not been a single underlying value across all stages of universal formation and maturation. There is every reason to consider the history of our universe with an understanding that **time changed as times changed.**

Einstein was the first to scientifically describe the malleable nature of time. However, that concept has been reflected in ancient scripture throughout the ages. The scriptural idea that a single day can be as a thousand years for God is not simply a poetic turn of phrase[18]. This reflects ancient awareness of the underlying realities of the heavens and earth. Pure energy is not bound by the constraints of time. For pure energy, there really is no difference between a single day and a thousand years, or a million years or billions upon billions of years.

---

[18] Psalms 90:4

Chapter 4. Einstein's Theory of Relativity

The Lorentz-Fitzgerald equations that correctly describe time dilation also apply to length and to mass as well. Figures 1 and 2 show the continuous operation of the correction equations for time, mass, and length across the full range of values below the speed of light.

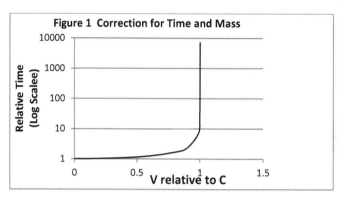

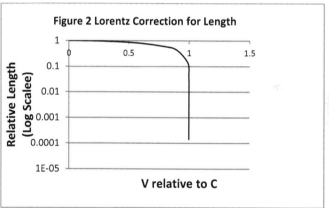

With increased speed, both corrected time and corrected mass increase, while corrected length decreases. The proportion of change is the same for all three units of measure because each correction is driven by the same mathematical function, the Fitzgerald ratio.

Below 90% the speed of light, the correction is very tiny and the slope of the correction curve is almost completely horizontal. Above 90% of the speed of light, the correction relationship approaches the vertical. At the exact speed of light, division or multiplication by zero applies for all corrections. Time and mass are undefined at the speed of light and the units of length shrink to nothing.

The up / down direction of the change is not as important to remember as is the fact that these changes are all real. The exact meanings of time, space, and matter are not constant but change according to the local conditions of speed or acceleration. Since gravitational pull is a condition of acceleration, each area of space experiences a correction for local gravity that changes the underlying values for mass, time, and space in that region. The physical attributes that we perceive as the firm scaffolding of this universe (matter, space, and time) are not at all firm but are different in every place and time.

The highly malleable nature of the scaffolding of our world supports a deeper and richer understanding of the true structure, function and mechanisms for formation of this universe. Pure energy and solid matter appear to represent two totally different things, but they both obey a single mathematical rule. Light, matter, space and time all are driven by the Fitzgerald ratio encoded into Lorentz correction equations. Albert Einstein looked at this circumstance and could not avoid the sense that this must mean something big, something really big. It does. What this means is that light and matter, which appear to be completely different things, are not really different. They are of the same essence. This is a fundamental meaning of Einstein's famous equation, $e=mc^2$.

The scientific equation, $e=mc^2$, has been introduced through popular communication so thoroughly that it is often declared to be the most well recognized equation in the world. However, its meaning has been less thoroughly communicated. Its full meaning is deeply reinforcing of faith in ways that have not been effectively taught.

Ancient scripture claims that this universe had a beginning. Faith holds that this material world is not simply a rearrangement of preexisting material, but a product of the creation of something from nothing. Einstein's famous equation shows that *creatio ex nihilo* has a solid foundation in modern science. Without justification, 20th century scientific educators have not broadly communicated this truth. We will begin to fill that gap.

The math behind e=mc^2 is not beyond our reach so we will not narrate around it; we will embrace it. Indeed, if you are still reading, you have already embraced it because the Lorentz-Fitzgerald equation for time dilation leads directly to Einstein's formula, e=mc^2. Using a technique that avoids calculus we can rearrange these correction equations to derive Einstein's famous equation, **e=mc^2**. From this work a very deep understanding of the structure and function of our world unfolds.

Details of the Lorentz-Fitzgerald equations are not presented in most popularized science summaries such as those written by Stephen Hawking. These high-level experts assume that non-experts cannot handle math – any math. The truth is that the math need not be addressed at the extremely advanced level required for the original discovery. Now that Einstein and others have completed the hard work, simpler mathematical models allow the average person to follow along. Using math not more difficult than 9th grade algebra, anyone can develop a robust understanding of key concepts such as:

- The complete interdependence of mass, time and space
- One method of derivation of Einstein's equation e=mc^2
- Why Einstein concluded that travel faster than the speed of light was impossible, and
- What might be true if Einstein was wrong (what might be true if faster than light travel does occur).

The Fitzgerald ratio incorporated into the Lorentz correction equations provides the basis for appreciating the details and nuances of these topics.

The Lorentz-Fitzgerald equations describe a natural mechanism reflecting simplicity of design linked to astoundingly complex results. These equations work like a 4-step computer program but these equations were not programmed by human engineers. These equations were discovered, not invented. They describe the way nature works, and nature works this way whether humanity appreciates the details or not.

Equations 1 and 1.1 show the Lorentz-Fitzgerald equations for the correction of time and mass at all values for actual speed. The correction for length works in the same general way as that for time, but yields values that get smaller when corrections for time and mass get larger.

Equation 1 Lorentz-Fitzgerald Correction for Time

$$t' = \left(\frac{t}{\sqrt{1 - \frac{v^2}{c^2}}} \right)$$

Equation 1.1 Lorentz-Fitzgerald Correction for Mass

$$m' = \left(\frac{m}{\sqrt{1 - \frac{v^2}{c^2}}} \right)$$

Equation 2 Lorentz-Fitzgerald Correction for Length

$$l' = \left(l * \sqrt{1 - \frac{v^2}{c^2}} \right)$$

In these equations

t = time at rest, and t' = corrected time;
m = mass at rest, and m' = corrected mass;
l = length at rest and l' = corrected length;
v = actual speed and
c = speed of light in a vacuum.

Actual speed compared to speed of light is the primary input parameter that determines the extent of the correction of time and length.

It might be helpful to glance again at Figures 1 and 2. The direction of change for length and mass is an increase while length is reduced with increased velocity. However, the patterns and proportion of change for each level of speed are the same for time, mass and length. The most prominent visual feature of these relationships is a j-hook showing abrupt change from almost horizontal (slow change) to nearly vertical (fast change) between 90% and 99% of the speed of light. This j-hook explains our routine perception that light and matter behave in completely different ways. Slow moving objects are described by the slow-changing (nearly horizontal) portion of the curves while the world of electrons is described by the fast-changing (nearly vertical) portion of the curve. Although rocks and electrons appear to behave according to completely different rules of physics, they actually obey a single, shared, mathematical rule.

The Mathematics of the Lorentz-Fitzgerald Equations

The appearance of complete separation of behavior between the extremes of light and matter involves a combination of four key steps. None of these four steps are individually complex, but their collective function is brilliant.

$$t' = \left(\frac{t}{\sqrt{1-\frac{v^2}{c^2}}} \right) \quad \text{Equation 1}$$

The first step, the step that determines the final outcome, is the calculation of ratio of the squares of actual speed of travel relative to the speed of light, v^2/c^2. At complete rest, that ratio calculates to a value of 0 because velocity is zero. When traveling at the full speed of light, the ratio calculates to a value of 1 because actual velocity is the same as the speed of light. Between those two extremes that ratio falls somewhere between 0 and 1.0. The square of the relative velocities amplifies the separation between slow moving objects (ratio around 0) verses those close to the speed of light (ratio around 1).

For instance, when the speed of travel is ½ that of the speed of light we get a 4-fold separation with a squared ratio of $\frac{1^2}{2^2} = \frac{1}{4}$. Slight additional slowing to 1/3 that of the speed of light yields a 9-fold separation ($\frac{1^2}{3^2} = \frac{1}{9}$). Additional slowing to 1/10 the speed of light yields a 100-fold separation for corrected values. Almost all of life in material form proceeds at less than 1/99.99 that of the speed of light so the mathematical separation between the apparent behavior for matter versus that of light is amplified more than 100 x 100 fold (more than 10,000 fold separation). This is one of the reasons why the slow moving world appears so different from the world at or near the speed of light.

$$t' = \left(\frac{t}{\sqrt{1 - \frac{v^2}{c^2}}} \right) \quad \text{Equation 1}$$

The second step in these important correction equations is the subtraction of the ratio we just calculated from the constant value, 1. The importance of this step may not immediately seem obvious but it is powerful and important to the world that we perceive. This subtraction step locks in the magnified separation introduced by squaring the ratio of v/c in the first step. The third step in the correction process will involve the taking of a square root of the intermediate results. Without this subtraction step, the magnification of the difference achieved by squaring the v/c ratio in Step 1 would be erased by the square root determination in Step 3. This subtraction step also causes the horizontal portion of this relationship to be associated with the relatively slow moving world of matter. If this was not the case, relativistic changes would be so dramatic that our clocks would change depending upon whether we walked or ran. Lastly, this subtraction step sets the stage for the absolute maximum speed for any travel or signal transmission within our personal spacetime.

The third step of the correction equation involves the calculation of the square root of the result of that subtraction step.

$$t' = \left(\frac{t}{\sqrt{subtraction\ step}} \right) \quad \text{Equation 1}$$

If v was ever greater than c, then the subtraction step would have yielded a negative value (the ratio of v2/c2 would be greater than 1). That means that the corrected value t' would equal the square root of a negative number. That is a real problem in math and this problem has deep implications. This problem explains why Einstein declared that nothing in this universe can travel faster than the speed of light. We will discuss this topic in greater detail in a later chapter.

As a fourth and final step, the result of that square root is either divided into uncorrected time or mass (to give corrected time or mass) or multiplied by uncorrected length (to give corrected length).

$$t' = \left(\frac{t}{3rd\ step\ result} \right)$$

$$m' = \left(\frac{m}{3rd\ step\ result} \right)$$

$$l' = (l * 3rd\ step\ result)$$

When the speed of travel is exactly the speed of light, the result of the second step will be zero, so the result of the third step will also be zero. At the speed of light, corrected values for mass and time will be a division by zero (mathematically undefined) and the fundamental unit for length will be a multiplication by zero (result always equals zero).

The final result of correction for relative speed follows one of 4 general outcome patterns:

1. Slow movement has a value for v^2/c^2 equal or nearly equal to zero. The subtraction step is very slight and the ultimate correction factor is imperceptibly different from the uncorrected value at rest.
2. Fast movement, above 90% of the speed of light, has a value for v^2/c^2 that approaches 1. The subtraction step drives that denominator close to zero, and that sets in motion very significant corrections. Even small incremental additions of speed drive extreme dilation of time or contraction of space.
3. At the exact speed of light the corrected value of length in the direction of travel becomes zero, and the corrected value for the duration of time or mass becomes mathematically undefined (1/zero).
4. At all speeds faster than the speed of light, the corrected value involves the square root of a negative number. Such a value is literally out of this world since the set of real numbers holds no value that is a square root for any negative number.

The correction for increased mass with acceleration follows the exact formula as that applied to time. Knowledge of this detail will support our deep dive into the most famous equation of all time.

The World's Most Famous Equation: $e = mc^2$

The most famous pronouncement of Einstein was the teaching of the interchangeability of energy and mass, through the relationship, $e=mc^2$. Prior to this point, all scientists viewed energy and matter as two completely different entities. The law for conservation of energy was seen as separate from the law of conservation of mass. According to Newton, energy could neither be created nor destroyed. In a similar way, matter could neither be created nor destroyed. Einstein changed this dual set of conservation laws. According to Einstein, it remained true that energy could never be created or destroyed, but matter might come and go like rain precipitating or vapor evaporating from or into the clouds. Einstein showed us that matter (mass) is simply another one of the multiple forms of the expression of energy. Chemical energy, kinetic energy, heat, electromagnetic radiation, potential energy, nuclear energy, **and mass** all represent specific manifestations of a single entity, energy.

No one in his day rivaled Einstein's ability to put the whole story together but Einstein's accomplishment was not a singular act of genius. Einstein's breakthrough was a demonstration of complete understanding and coordination of all known facts of his day. Important facts become lost when the retelling of Einstein's accomplishment focuses too much on the ingenious nature of his 'thought experiments.' The truth is that many laboratory scientists and mathematicians set the table for Einstein's feast of glory. Understanding his theory is best accomplished by understanding the preliminary work of those other scientists. Critical to Einstein's work was the confirmation of the absolute invariance of the speed of light coupled with multiple studies of fast moving matter like electrons and protons.

Sir Isaac Newton characterized the movement of solid matter and his equations had worked perfectly for nearly two centuries before the time of Einstein. However late 19th century studies of light and subatomic particles simply were not matching the expectations predicted by the physics of Newton. It turned out that Newton's physics apply adequately to the world of slow moving objects but fail to characterize the realm of the electron and other subatomic particles. Adding more energy to a slow moving object predictably leads to an increase in speed. That increase in speed is always proportional to the amount of additional energy, the mass of the moved object, and the starting velocity of the moved object.

For objects that we can see and touch, Newton allowed perfect predictions of how speed would change upon the addition of more energy. However, by the end of the 1800s, experiments conducted in separate laboratories had confirmed that fast moving objects like protons showed less than expected increase in speed with the addition of more energy. It was becoming apparent that the speed of light represented an absolute maximum speed limit. It was also becoming clear that Newton's laws of motion lost accuracy near that maximum speed limit. Experiments on subatomic particles were also starting to show a result that could have been mistaken as experimental error but for the fact that the error was not random. The unexpected "error" followed a consistent pattern. When a subatomic particle that was already traveling at a very high speed received additional energy, it did not gain additional speed but appeared to gain weight. How could that be? The law of conservation of energy declared that the added energy could not just disappear and the law of conservation of mass declared that new mass could not be created. These findings were very difficult to explain. However, these results must have meant something. They did, indeed, mean something.

The facts supporting that conclusion had been sitting in view of scientific observers for more than a decade, but it was Einstein who came to realize both the qualitative and quantitative meanings of those facts. The qualitative meaning was that **energy was being converted into mass rather than velocity**. The quantitative meaning would rely upon the ratio of that obscure Irish physicist who, in the 1880s, claimed that the electrons became shorter in the direction of travel near the speed of light. The ratio originally published by Fitzgerald, $\sqrt{1 - v^2/c^2}$, exactly described the proportion by which new mass was gained in studies of charged particles shot through smoke clouds.

Starting with the Lorentz-Fitzgerald correction equations for mass (the same as that which applies to time), Einstein developed his famous equation for the interconversion of mass and energy, e=mc². Einstein realized that the amount of gained mass was related to those correction equations. Those equations required knowledge of a starting mass and a velocity of travel. Newton's equations for kinetic energy involved a function of an amount of mass traveling at a particular velocity. Einstein sensed that he might be able to pull those general relationships together. He sensed correctly. Einstein started with the equations of the Lorentz-Fitzgerald corrections and used those equations to model how much mass changed upon adding new energy. From there, he was able to rearrange the Lorentz-Fitzgerald equations to interface with Newton's equations for kinetic energy. In that way, Einstein was able to show how changes in mass predicted by the Lorentz-Fitzgerald corrections aligned with Newton's equations for kinetic energy. Pulling all of this together, Einstein became the first human to recognize that e=mc^2.

You and I might never have thought to do what Einstein did if we had lived in his day. Hundreds of true geniuses of his day did not. However, I can assure you that we can follow what he did and we can understand it.

It is not easy for non-experts to read and understand Einstein's direct teachings on relativity theory. Einstein actually attempted a popularized summary of relativity theory but even this is not simple to follow.[19] He points to his reliance upon the Lorentz-Fitzgerald equations, but he did not show an easy way to follow along with his derivation of e=mc^2. My search for details on the method for this derivation routinely pointed to methods involving calculus because this is a very good way of studying rate of change (like the gain of new mass). However, most people will not enjoy following a derivation method involving calculus. Instead, I found an intriguing alternative technique summarized in the 1960s by the prolific writer, Isaac Asimov.

Most of the math that follows is within our reach using 9th grade algebra. One exception is the use of an advanced algebraic rearrangement of terms using Newton's binomial theory, a technique not used by the average person today. Before electronic calculators, Newton's method provided a practical way to solve

---

[19] Einstein, Albert. <u>Relativity. The Special and the General Theory. A Popular Exposition; A Clear Explanation That Anyone Can Understand.</u> Translated by Robert W Lawson. 1961, Crown Publishers, Inc. New York, ISBN 0517025302.

complicated square roots of the type required by the Lorentz-Fitzgerald equation. A person like Einstein would have been well versed in this rearrangement technique. Although we will not derive the binomial theorem rearrangement, we can show how this method could have helped bring about the original observation that energy and mass were equivalent per the function, e=mc².

The Asimov technique starts with acknowledgement that all moving objects have kinetic energy. The equation for kinetic energy as a function of mass and velocity of any object was taught to the world by Newton and this equation is a critical feature of Einstein's final determination that e = mc². As such, we should review a few details regarding kinetic energy.

Kinetic energy is the amount of energy reflected by the movement of any object. That energy tends to keep an object moving until it is redirected by contact with something else. When an object hits an obstacle, it transfers kinetic energy to the impacted object. That energy can either rebound back (like a bouncing ball) or it can be absorbed by another object (as with a billiard ball accelerated by the impact of another). The transfer of kinetic energy from any moving object depends upon how massive the object is, and upon how fast it is traveling. Just as was the case for outward drift in the corners for NASCAR racers, kinetic energy is higher for heavier objects and for faster objects. For objects that we can see and feel, kinetic energy changes according to a very precise formula. Newton's equation for kinetic energy is shown in Equation 3 below.

Equation 3: Kinetic Energy of Moving Object

$$e = \frac{1}{2}m\,v^2 \quad \text{Equation 3}$$

In Equation 3, **v** is the velocity of travel and **m** is the mass of the object. The result, **e**, is the kinetic energy of the moving mass. Consistent with our perception of the world, the kinetic energy of a projectile increases with higher speed and with higher mass.

As with all equations, rearrangement is possible by following the rules of making equal changes to both sides of the equation. An example rearrangement of Newton's classic form is shown in Equation 4 below.

Equation 4: Rearranged Equation for Kinetic Energy

$$v^2 = \frac{2e}{1m}\text{, or}$$

$$v = \sqrt{\frac{2e}{m2e}} \quad \text{Equation 4}$$

(error corrected Feb 2020)

This type of rearrangement would have been used in cloud chamber experiments. The scientists would have known the starting mass of the subatomic particle and they would have known the energy input into the experiment. They could then calculate the velocity that they would have expected to achieve. It was this number that fell short in actual experiments. That shortfall is what started the process that we are going to now follow. Following this type of rearrangement process we will move through a step-by-step process to show how the Lorentz-Fitzgerald equations can be linked up with Newton's equation for energy as a function of mass and velocity. As we proceed, I urge you avoid any expectation that we should immediately realize how and why Einstein did what he did. This exercise does not require us to think like Einstein. We can understand the meaning of this area of science even if we don't reinvent it. All we need do is to follow along with the process of rearrangements that Einstein would have expected to be possible and helpful.

As we go along we will use basic rules of algebra to rearrange equations from one form into an equivalent restatement. This might be a good time to review and really understand why these mathematical relationships are called EQUAtions. They are called EQUAtions, because they are EQUAL on both sides and that means that they can be reorganized into other forms that are also EQUAL on both sides. We can restate equivalent statements using other equivalent statements. We can cause equivalent statements to take on slightly different formats regarding the way in which elements of the equation appear. In the process of rearrangement using the rules of algebra, the middle stages might look a little messy. In the end, a final rearrangement or two will shake that messiness out and the final answer will emerge in front of our eyes, looking not at all messy. Rearrangement is what algebra is all about. Algebra is the process of rearranging messy looking equations until we see the answer sitting clearly in front of our eyes. That is what Einstein did.

As we work through these rearrangements, I know that it will be tempting to declare that "I just don't understand!" I have experienced this, and I have seen this in others. As I aged I came to understand something that might help you if you think you do not understand. Often, the problem really isn't that we don't understand the rules, or any specific step taken according to those rules. The problem is that we don't immediately recognize why or how the teacher came to think of taking that specific step at that specific time. Especially, in the case of Einstein's work, do not let that stop you. Do not allow yourself to be derailed by self-doubt about whether you would have personally thought to make the rearrangements that Einstein did. It doesn't matter. Einstein was surrounded by elite scientists who had access to all the same facts and still did not think to do what Einstein did! That is why he is considered as a genius. The truth is that you and I can follow what he did, and we can come to understand what it means, even if we would have never figured it out on our own. To understand this topic of science, we don't need to chart the way. We just need to follow the map.

Equation 5: Lorentz-Fitzgerald Equation for Correction of Mass

The expansion of mass with additional energy follows the Lorentz-Fitzgerald correction equation in the exact pattern applicable to time dilation. This is reflected in Equation 5.

$$M1 = M0 \left(\frac{1}{\sqrt{1-\frac{v^2}{c^2}}} \right) \quad \text{Equation 5}$$

The original mass of the subatomic particle is reflected as **M0** and the mass corrected for acceleration is **M1**. The overall process that we are going to follow is to determine the difference between **M1** and **M0** caused by the addition of new energy. That difference (small case, **m**) is the mass equivalence of the energy added to the experiment. The discovery that e=mc^2 is really not more complicated than that.

Now, we just start the process of rearranging equations to get there. Let us focus again on Equation 5 which is shown below in a classic form for Lorentz-Fitzgerald correction for mass given the details of actual velocity. M1 is the corrected mass given that M0 was any given original mass driven to any given velocity (v).

$$M1 = M0 \left(\frac{1}{\sqrt{1-\frac{v^2}{c^2}}} \right) \quad \text{Equation 5}$$

We can see this equation, and we can understand how to work it when we have a specific value for actual velocity (v). However, Einstein was not looking for an answer that applied to only a specific set of experimental data. He sensed that his answer should be generally applied across all values of actual velocity. So, he needed to solve this problem without giving any specific value to the term, **v**. However, when trying to rearrange these equations using a generalized term for v, that messy square root in a denominator will cause more than a little difficulty. This difficulty can be avoided by using knowledge of the rules for exponents. Equation 5 can be rearranged into the form of Equation 6 using the algebraic rules for exponents.

$$M1 = M0 \left(1 - \frac{v^2}{c^2}\right)^{-1/2} \quad \text{Equation 6}$$

Dividing by a square root is the same as raising any term to the power of negative one-half. That rule is applied to rearrange Equation 5 into Equation 6. That rearrangement allows us to take advantage of an old technique in math, one that is not used often today but was critical in the days before electronic calculators.

The rearrangement shown as Equation 6 takes on the general form $(1 - b)^{-a}$ Look at Eq. 6.1 below compared to Eq 6.

$$M1 = M0(1 - b)^{-a} \quad \text{Equation 6.1}$$

In our case, $b = \frac{v^2}{c^2}$ and the exponent term is $-a = -\frac{1}{2}$.

$$M1 = M0 \left(1 - \frac{v^2}{c^2}\right)^{-1/2} \quad \text{Equation 6}$$

Recognizing that the Lorentz-Fitzgerald correction equations can be arranged in the form of Equation 6.1 could have allowed Einstein to recognize the applicability of a tool first taught by Sir Isaac Newton. (This is not a tool used in high school math today, but we can follow how it could have been used.) As taught by Sir Isaac Newton, complex square roots of the form $(1 - b)^{-a}$ can be solved by a process that involves only additions and multiplications. This is called an 'infinite series' addition technique. The answer to the square root is approached as successively better approximations attained by adding a series of successive numbers, Term 1 + Term 2 + Term 3 ... etc, theoretically continuing through an infinite number of terms to achieve greater and greater levels of precision in the final answer. The first term gives a starting point, the second term gives an important adjustment relative to Term 1, and then Terms 3, 4, 5, etc., provide continuously smaller incremental improvements to the approximation. When you know how to do it, calculation of each individual term and adding of those terms is easier than calculation of a complicated square root. As a scientist trained in the 18th century, Einstein would have known this method.

For our function in the form of $(1 - b)^{-a}$ the first three successive terms are:

1. Term 1= exactly 1.0
2. Term 2 = ab (a times b) which is always less than 1
3. Term 3 = $(a^2 + a)*b^2$ BUT WE WON'T NEED IT.

For our Lorentz-Fitzgerald correction, $b = \frac{v^2}{c^2}$ and $-a = -\frac{1}{2}$. Of course the value of positive a is $= +\frac{1}{2}$.

So for our calculation:

Term 1 will be exactly 1.0 and

Term 2 will be $(a * b)$ or $\frac{1}{2} \times \frac{v^2}{c^2}$ or $\frac{v^2}{2c^2}$.

Term 3 will be not needed.

Our answer will be adequately calculated using Only Terms 1 and 2 and ignoring Terms 3, 4 and higher. This is how it works.

Equation 7: Rearranged Correction for Gained Mass

The Lorentz-Fitzgerald Equation for corrected mass, M1, is shown in the form of Equation 6 and restated in the general form of Equation 6.1 in order to prepare us to use Newton's method for square roots.

$$M1 = M0 \left(1 - \frac{v^2}{c^2}\right)^{-1/2} \text{ Equation 6}$$

$$M1 = M0 * (1 - b)^{-a} \text{ Equation 6.1}$$

Taking advantage of Newton's binomial theory we can rearrange Equation 6.1 to yield Equation 7.0.

$$M1 = M0 * (\text{Term 1} + \text{Term 2}) \quad \text{Equation 7.0}$$

When we substitute the vales for Term 1 (the constant = 1) and Term 2 $(\frac{v^2}{2c^2})$ as worked out above, we get Equation 7.1.

$$M1 = M0\left(1 + \frac{v^2}{2c^2}\right) \quad \text{Equation 7.1}$$

Once rearranged to form Equation 7.1, we can remove ourselves from the details of Newton's binomial theory and return to familiar steps for arithmetic and algebra. We achieve Equation 7.2 by using the distributive property of multiplication. We distribute M0 into the parentheses by multiplying $M0$ with both Term 1 and Term 2. Equation 7.2 shows this step.

$$M1 = \left(M0 * 1 + \frac{M0 * v^2}{2c^2}\right) \quad \text{Equation 7.2}$$

Before we move on, let me be sure that we are clear about what these abbreviations mean.

> M1 stands for new mass corrected for high speed travel,
>
> M0 stands for original mass, and
>
> m stands for mass created $(M1 - M0)$
>
> v2 = the square of actual velocity (any velocity)
>
> c2 = the square of the speed of light.

With this preliminary work, we can now begin the step-wise solution for the value of m (small m) which is the amount of mass created by the addition of new energy.

> *Step 1:* m = (M1 − M0).

Here we face an equation that has too many variables to be easily solved. We need an equation that has one variable representing our answer (m) and only one other variable (either M1 or M0). This is not a big problem because we know how to restate M1 in terms of M0.

Look at equation 7.2 which states M1 (left side) in terms of M0 (right side). We can substitute the right side of equation 7.2 any place that we would otherwise need to know the value for M1.

$$M1 = \left(M0 * 1 + \frac{M0 * v^2}{2c^2}\right) \quad \text{Equation 7.2}$$

Remember that we are ultimately solving for m, small m, the amount of new mass formed. We solve for small *m* by finding the difference between *M1* and *M0*. However, we need to state that subtraction using only one of those two variables (either variable named M1 or variable named M0 but not both). We can do this by replacing the term, *M1* by its equivalent function stated in terms of *M0* as in Eq. 7.2, right side.

Step 2 shows that small *m* equals the difference of M1 — M0 which equals a function of *M0* without ever again needing the term, M1.

$$Step\ 2:\ m = M1 - M0 = \left(M0 + \frac{M0v^2}{2c^2}\right) - M0$$

Step 3 shows the simplification of the far right side of that equation by simply dropping the parentheses and subtracting like terms. (*M0* subtracts from *M0* to leave zero plus a messy multiplication and division term.)

$$Step\ 3:\ m = 0 + \frac{M0 * v^2}{2c^2}$$

Let us rearrange Step 3 because this will show how close we are getting to a match with the structure of Newton's classic equation for kinetic energy.

$$Rearranged\ Step\ 3:\ m = \left(\frac{1}{2} * M0 * v^2 * 1/c^2\right)$$

$$Equation\ 3\ Kinetic\ Energy:\ e = \frac{1}{2} * m * v^2$$

In rearranged Step 3, we have ½, times our starting mass, times actual velocity squared, times the reciprocal of the speed of light squared ($1/c^2$). That almost matches the format of the Newton's equation for kinetic energy, which says that energy equals ½, times a mass, times actual velocity squared.

Yes, in rearranged Step 3 we still have an extra term, the reciprocal of the speed of light squared ($1/c^2$). That term does not fit perfectly into Newton's formal equation, but we are getting close. In Step 4 we clean up the equation for Step 3. We clean up the right side of the equation by taking advantage of the fact that the multiplication by $1/c^2$ is the same as division by c^2.

$$Step\ 4:\quad m = \tfrac{1}{2}\ M0\ v^2 \div c^2$$

We have also dropped the inserted multiplication signs (*) because we know that any two terms placed adjacent to each other represent an intended multiplication.

Now, we can move that freestanding term c^2 from the right side of the equation to the left side by multiplying both sides by c^2.

$$Step\ 5:\quad m * c^2 = \left(\tfrac{1}{2}\ M0\ v^2\right)$$

Let's look again at Newton's equation for kinetic energy.

$$Equation\ 3:\quad e = \frac{1}{2}m\,v^2$$

Do you see how the definition of kinetic energy matches the right side of Step 5? The right side of the equation in Step 5 is the same as Newton's formula for kinetic energy. One-half, times mass, times velocity squared. Because equals can be substituted for equals, we could just substitute the abbreviation for kinetic energy, e, in place of the right side of the equation in Step 5. That gives us the form shown in Step 6 below.

$$Step\ 6:\ mc^2 = e$$

Let's switch the left / right orientation of Step 6 to get:

$$Step\ 7:\quad e = mc^2.$$

You have just derived Einstein's famous equation!

Starting with the recognition that acceleration of a subatomic particle caused a smaller than expected increase in speed, the scientists of Einstein's day went on to document that they were observing a gain in mass instead. The difference between the new mass and the original mass is the amount of mass gained. The rate of gained mass can be calculated using the Lorentz-Fitzgerald equation. Subtracting the original mass from the new mass shows the amount of new mass gained. Scientists knew how much energy they put in and Einstein correctly deduced that this energy must have been converted into the amount of mass gained. That concept, plus step-by-step rearrangements of equations using some basic rules of algebra (plus one antique process for manually solving square roots) allows us to see the quantitative relationship for defining the energy equivalence of mass.

Do not feel flustered when considering that you might not have thought to do the steps shown here. Almost no one would. That was part of the genius of Einstein. The key is that now that he has done it, we can understand how it's done. Now you understand how a key finding of the relativity theory was derived. You also understand why it has been called the theory of **relativity**. The starting point for understanding that e=mc^2 is the understanding of the Lorentz-Fitzgerald corrections. These equations show that time, mass and length are not absolute values, but are **relative values**. The actual value for the underlying units of time, matter, and space are defined by the local conditions of actual velocity of travel **relative to the velocity of light**.

In full disclosure, the process that we just followed does not give Einstein's complete equation for the equivalence between mass and energy. However, the public has almost never been exposed to Einstein's full equation even though it is not a difficult detail to understand. Einstein's equation viewed in its most common form, **e=mc^2**, is exactly accurate only at complete rest. Literally, it declares the **rest equivalence** of energy and matter. When an object is in motion, that simplified equation is only an approximation. The more precise equation is e = mc^2 + **R** (**R** = a remainder). The value of that remainder increases with additional speed such that the precise and formal declaration of Einstein's equation is

$$e = mc^2 + \left(\frac{1}{2} * m * \frac{v^2}{c^2} \right)$$

Luckily, we need not do the calculations for this remainder term, but I bet that you recognize a ratio that links back to the Fitzgerald ratio. If in our derivation process we would have included the infinite series terms 3, 4 and higher, we would have shown the impact of that remainder. However, that would have made the derivation steps more difficult and would typically yield only minor adjustments to the precise calculation of the energy equivalence of mass in motion. At or below 40% light-speed (120,000 km per second) the remainder error is less than 1.0% the total value. Almost all the energy equivalence of mass is in the form of its rest mass. That is one of the reasons that the energy delivered by tapping into nuclear energy is so extreme.

What Does This Mean?

One of the obvious meanings of this chapter is that a working knowledge of science is not beyond our reach. The atheists are wrong when they declare that the faithful are ignorant. The faithful can master scientific understanding at a sophisticated level! Faith is not a result of ignorance because faith and science are not at odds!

We have covered the essential details of time dilation, length contraction, and interconversion of energy and mass. We have covered the details that erase any argument against the possibility of *creatio ex nihilo*. We have covered the fact that the origin of God needs no explanation beyond that expected for energy. I have to ask those who believe that logic and reason have no room for faith in God, "What part of this area of modern science rules out the possibility of God?" The true answer to this question is that nothing of the science of the 20th and 21st centuries argues against the possibility of God. The more a person understands about science, the more clearly one sees that faith and science are not at odds. Those who believe that science has debunked God have been misled. Those who pass that idea along, mislead.

Prior to Einstein, the physics taught by Newton prevented many well educated scientists from believing in a Creator. Those with advanced scientific training in the 19th century mistakenly thought that matter could not be created. It seemed reasonable that creation could not have taken place, therefore the idea of a Creator was at odds with science. However, that 19th century interpretation of science has been proven wrong! Beginning with relativity theory, modern science has reestablished full concordance between science and faith in our Creator.

Even those who are not elite scientists can thoroughly understand that light and matter appear to be two different things even though they are not really different. Matter is a product of light. From pure energy, matter can take form. That means that faith in *creatio ex-nihilo*, 'creation from nothing', is supported by modern science. We have seen that an immaterial God can be understood as a prime cause without need for a further cause, just as energy is without need of a further cause. We can understand that the theological concepts of omnipresence, timelessness, transcendence beyond time, and a beginning of time, are all consistent with the facts of modern science.

The truth is that modern science does not conflict with faith. **Modern science conflicts with atheism.** The scientific leadership of the 18th and 19th centuries might have claimed a scientific rationale for adopting atheism over faith in God, but modern atheism enjoys absolutely no support from the facts of modern science. The truth is that atheism continues today only through distortion and falsification of the relationship between the facts of science and the fundamental elements of faith in God. Atheism continues today as a system of beliefs driven by preconceived bias, not by the facts of science.

The foundation that we have developed to this point has prepared us to delve deeply into the examination of the match between modern science and faith in God. In the next two chapters we will examine the concordance between the facts of modern science and the creative steps taught since antiquity through the first of God's faithful, the Hebrews. We will find that modern science gives us every reason to pursue a greater understanding of the God of the Bible, the Creator who introduced Himself to humanity simply as,

"I Am."

Chapter 5. Light is the Fundamental 'Atomos'

"Let there be light" was the first declarative act of creation and this ancient declaration finds complete support in the facts of modern science. There currently is no doubt that our universe had a beginning. This beginning truly involved a formless void, with no matter, no space and no time. The first active step was the emergence of light, electromagnetic radiation. That first light served as the raw material for everything else.

Armed with a working knowledge of the Lorentz-Fitzgerald equations and Einstein's equation, $e=mc^2$, you have the foundations for understanding the role of light as the raw material for every fleck of matter in this universe. This chapter and the next will examine key details of that transformation from pure energy into all that makes up this material world.

Figure 1 Electromagnetic Spectrum (aka, Light)[20]

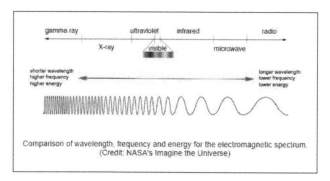

Comparison of wavelength, frequency and energy for the electromagnetic spectrum. (Credit: NASA's Imagine the Universe)

Light is just another word for electromagnetic radiation (EMR) which is the fluctuating waveform of electric and magnetic fields transmitted through space. Light is more than the relatively narrow band of wavelengths that humans can see. Light is a full spectrum of electromagnetic radiation ranging from very short wavelength

---

[20] Electromagnetic waves (radiation): "Another term for light. Light waves are fluctuations of electric and magnetic fields in space". Source: NASA. http://imagine.gsfc.nasa.gov/resources/dict_ei.html#em_waves. Viewed 12/28/14

radiation (high energy) to very long wavelength radiation (low energy). The full spectrum of light is diagramed in Figure 1. The full spectrum of light (EMR) includes gamma rays, X-rays, ultraviolet light, human-visible light, infrared light, radio waves, and microwaves. Gamma rays and X-rays represent examples of very high-energy light. Microwaves and radio waves represent examples of very low energy light. Light which is visible to sighted humans is simply a narrow band in the mid-range of this energy spectrum. Different zones of this energy spectrum interact with solid matter in different ways but the various levels of energy within the electromagnetic spectrum are not different entities. All frequencies of this energy spectrum are 'light' and they all share the common feature of travel at exactly the same velocity, the "c" of $e=mc^2$.

Electricity and magnetism were once thought to represent two different forces of nature, but we now know that electricity and magnetism reflect a single type of energy. Mathematically, both of these forces satisfy the same complete set of physical equations so scientists consider them merged as a single type of energy. That merger of electricity and magnetism is called 'electromagnetic radiation.' Not all energy measurable today can be directly classified as electromagnetic radiation. However, there are good reasons to think that all current energy types are reflections of a common pool of energy which was merged as one common force in the beginning. As the nuclear age unfolded, we learned of two types of force, the strong and the weak nuclear forces that hold atomic nuclei together. While appearing as separate types of energy, the best evidence of modern science points to the expectation that the nuclear forces and electromagnetic radiation were merged into a single common energy pool under the very hot conditions of the early universe. These nuclear forces demonstrated unique characteristics upon the formation of the first atomic nuclei, but these forces were not distinct until well into the progression toward the formation of nuclear elements. Physicists now talk of the 'electroweak force' as the merger of the nuclear forces with electromagnetic radiation under the very energetic conditions of the first microsecond(s) of this universe. Gravity appears to represent another separate force of nature, but Einstein's generalized theory of relativity demonstrates a full merger of gravity and electromagnetism under one important condition. If some of the more advanced equations of Einstein's relativity theory are calculated with the assumption that our world has at least five dimensions of spacetime, then gravity and electromagnetism behave as a common, merged force. The implications of this finding regarding the structure of a more complicated universe will be discussed in a later chapter. For now, the point is that we are scientifically justified to view all forces and materials of this universe as variations upon a common pool of immaterial energy.

The idea of light as the fundamental raw material for everything else could not have been fathomed in the absence of relativity theory. That idea is now inescapable. However, while the details are thoroughly modern, the general idea is actually quite old. Since antiquity, scientifically minded thinkers expected that future developments would reveal an underlying common element that serves as a fundamental building block for all other things. Around 500 BC the Greek philosopher, Democratis, used the word "Atomos" (meaning "un-cuttable") to describe this theorized fundamental building block. The thought was that this invisible and uncuttable building block would be combined in various patterns to make everything else.

During the 17th through 19th centuries, chemists thought that they had discovered these uncuttable building blocks in the form of the elements of the periodic table. The atomic elements such as hydrogen, oxygen, carbon, nitrogen, and the rest of more

than 92 elements appeared to represent uncuttable basic building blocks. That is why they were called, atoms. We still call these elements, 'atoms,' today, even though we have found that each of these elements can be cut into more fundamental building blocks called protons, neutrons, and electrons. Still further progress in the 20th century has shown that even those subatomic particles are made of even smaller particles called quarks. It is possible that quarks are made of something even more fundamental.

As we focus on smaller and smaller fundamental particles we approach the exact interface between pure energy and the most fundamental particles of matter. The exact form of matter that exists at the exact interface between pure energy and matter would be of such high energy that we would not expect to find any of it around to touch and to hold. These material forms would represent transitional structure(s), quickly morphing to other forms that are longer lasting. Although we should not expect to find a stable example of the type of matter that directly precipitates from pure energy, we should be able to generate examples of that type of matter for fleeting intervals under conditions of very high energy. Indeed, scientists have recently achieved success along those lines.

The Large Hadron Collider in Europe has smashed subatomic particles against each other at the highest energies yet created in the laboratory. From extremely high energy subatomic collisions, scientists appear to have finally produced a short-lived subatomic particle thought to have directly precipitated from pure energy at the beginning of time. Fifty years before its first experimental production in 2012, theoretical physicist, Peter Higgs predicted the existence of a type of particle that would be of very high energy and very short lived, disintegrating almost immediately into the more stable quarks that go on to form electrons, protons and neutrons. That particle has been named the Higgs Boson in his honor. It also carries the flippant nickname, 'The God Particle,' reflecting its importance as the point of origin for all other subatomic particles[21]. That very basic subatomic particle is of such high energy that its creation in the laboratory mandated careful attention to ensuring that its energy could be fully controlled and extinguished once produced. (The full energy of such a particle could be sufficiently great as to trigger a chain reaction destabilizing all of creation if released into the wild.)

Whether the Higgs Boson is alone or whether there are additional unstable particles at the exact interface between pure energy and solid matter is not yet resolved. However, this detail is not critical for an overall understanding of the origin of this universe. There may be any number of sub-subatomic particles on the material side of the interface between energy and matter. Whatever those details are, it is clear that this interface is characterized by the relationship, $e = mc^2$. We have the capacity to understand Einstein's declaration of the transmutability of energy and matter ($e = mc^2$). We also have the capacity to fully understand the operations of the Lorentz-Fitzgerald equations. With this foundation, we are prepared to understand important dynamics regarding the first microseconds of the formation of this universe.

There are good reasons to view the interconversion between energy and matter as a phase change, like the precipitation of snowflakes from the vapor in cold air. The first physical realization of Einstein's equation $e = mc^2$ was the phase change from pure energy into solidified matter. Just as snow is separated from vapor based upon a new physical characteristic (a change in density), newly transformed matter would also take on some important new characteristic. It is reasonable to expect that newly formed matter separated from pure energy on the basis of speed of travel. Once transformed from pure energy, mass (matter) must travel slower than 'c', enforcing

---

[21] Leon Lederman with Dick Teresi. The God Particle Dell Publishing, New York, 1993. ISBN 0385312113

real-number valuations for space and for time according to the Lorentz-Fitzgerald equations.

The Big Bang

The theoretical plausibility for a created universe brought forth by transformation of pure energy into matter is a direct product of Einstein's theory of relativity. However, as a staunch atheist, Einstein resisted any jump to concluding that this universe actually had a beginning. Until well after Einstein's death, atheists argued that this universe did not have a beginning at all. It turned out that the atheistic argument was wrong. It turns out that there is no longer any basis for arguing against a universal creation event just like the one attributed to the God of the ancient Hebrews.

The truth is that this universe did have a beginning. It originated about 13.8 billion years ago. In the beginning there was no matter, no time, and no space. Suddenly, abruptly, there was electromagnetic radiation – light – and a lot of it. From a starting point with no space, space burst forth like the opening of a parachute. Space took form because matter took form. Along with space, time also had its beginnings as a secondary product of the precipitation of matter. The scientific knowledge regarding the beginning and maturation of our material universe reads as a full confirmation of the scriptural claims of Genesis Chapter 1.

The first confirmed signal that our universe had a beginning was the determination that our universe is expanding. An expanding universe must have once been smaller. The rollback to smaller size in past times can continue only as far as the point at which the volume of space rolls all the way back to zero. In the beginning, our universe had zero units of space. That is exactly the condition that we would expect if the starting point involved the precipitous formation of new matter as a phase change from pure energy with no preexisting matter before that phase change.

Light is the Fundamental 'Atomos'

In 1929, Edwin Hubble (namesake of the Hubble Telescope) started a change in scientific understanding that would not be reversed. In that year, Hubble announced his findings that all distant galaxies demonstrated a 'red shift.

> Red shift for light is the equivalent of the familiar Doppler Effect which is the "EEEEEE-UMMMMM" sound change that we hear when fast moving machines approach and then pass us. Compared to the steady pitch of sound heard by the pilot, a stationary person hears a fast moving machine with a higher pitch while approaching with a quick change to a lower pitch when moving away. Traveling at a fixed speed, sound waves tend to stack up as the machine approaches and stretch out as the machine departs. For light emitted from objects moving away from us, the light wave cycles become stretched out. For light, stretched wave cycles shifts color toward the red side of the spectrum.

A red shift is a shifting to a more red color of the spectrum of light sent from distant galaxies. The amount of red shift follows a steady mathematical pattern, with greater red shifts demonstrated by galaxies that are farther away. Since light can never travel faster or slower than c, this finding can only be explained by the stretching out of the light rays, with a resulting appearance of a longer wave length. That explanation can only occur if there is a literal expansion of space, a stretching out of the unit of space between galaxies. That is truly happening. Galaxies of this universe are drifting farther apart because the space between them is being stretched out.

Although Hubble is forever credited as the discoverer of the expanding universe, he was not the first to demonstrate this finding. Others before Hubble had reported 'red shift' and had interpreted that as a sign of the expanding universe. However, it took the international reputation of a man like Hubble to convince critics like Albert Einstein that our universe was indeed expanding. As early as 1912, a little known astronomer named Vesto Slipher documented a red shift from the Andromeda Galaxy. Slipher's 1912 finding was truly novel but not understood. It was dismissed as unimportant. Then, in 1919, Einstein's general theory of relativity included equations that predicted an expanding universe. Allowing his atheistic bias to overwhelm the evidence in front of him, Einstein actually disbelieved this detail of his new theory. In order to avoid supporting any notion of an expanding universe, Einstein published his General Theory of Relativity with a mathematical fudge factor called the "cosmological constant." This factor served no purpose other than cancelling out the mathematical signals of an expanding universe. In 1927, Monsignor Georges Lemaître, a Roman Catholic priest who was also an accomplished physicist, published a paper with calculations reconciling Einstein's work with the prior efforts of Slipher. Lemaître concluded that the red shifts seen by Slipher represented the physical stretching out of space predicted by Einstein's unadjusted equations. Initially ignored, Lemaître's work gained scientific credibility two years later when Edwin Hubble drew the same conclusion. Hubble's work provided direct evidence of red shift, not just from isolated locations as presented by Slipher, but from all distant stars in all directions throughout the universe. Hubble's work confirmed that all galaxies were moving away from all other galaxies. Every point in space is moving away from every other point in space with no special central point.

In an age of receptivity to scientific discovery, including the embrace of concepts such as the malleable nature of time and space, why did the topic of an expanding universe generate intense resistance? Why would Einstein actually 'dry lab' an adjustment to his most important work in rejection of any signal that the universe was expanding? The answer to this lies in theology and prejudice, not science and measurement. Recall that atheism grew among scientists based upon Newton's conservation laws which argued against the possibility of a creation event. Einstein's original paper in 1905 demonstrated that creation was theoretically possible ($e=mc^2$) but did not conclude that it had actually occurred. Einstein's second paper on general relativity actually showed that the universe should be considered an expanding universe but Einstein ignored that signal. You see, an expanding universe suggested a creation event and Einstein did not believe in a creation event. This was one of the first confirmed demonstrations of a scientific leader twisting scientific facts to fit a personal adoption of atheism as a matter of anti-faith prioritized over fact.

Over the next half century, atheists who resisted the concept of a created universe continued to argue in favor of alternative explanations. These arguments have now been overwhelmed by repeated addition of new evidence that continually reinforced the conclusion that our universe did indeed have a beginning. The first step of that beginning was the emergence of light which, then, formed matter.

The emergence of pure light as the precursor to matter, space and time is now called, "The Big Bang." Originally resisted by atheistic leaders in the science community, the validity of the Big Bang mechanism is now undeniable on the basis of multiple levels of evidence. Physicists predicted that if pure light was the original source of the matter held by this universe, then one would expect a sign in the form of some universally distributed residual energy. Physicists were able to predict some specific characteristics that this residual energy should demonstrate. Although the initial burst of energy would have been hotter than the sun, the residue of that initial energy would now be measurable as a very low frequency energy wave with a very low associated temperature. This is because its wavelength would have been stretched out due to universal expansion of space since the beginning. It would have now cooled to a temperature just a few degrees warmer than the absolute zero temperature (that would be just a few degrees warmer than negative 273 degrees centigrade). Furthermore, this residual radiation would be distributed evenly throughout all areas of space. Beginning in 1964, these scientific predictions started receiving one independent confirmation after another.

In 1964, Arno Penzias and Robert Wilson of Bell Laboratories were working on a highly sensitive radio telescope and could not resolve a problem with a very tenacious source of low energy electrical interference. Regardless of the technique used to shield their devices against electrical interference, they could never free their experiment from a very low level of electronic background noise. No matter which area of the sky was the subject of that day's focus, their radio telescopes always recorded that low level of electromagnetic static. Although it was another team of scientists who correctly interpreted the meaning of this unavoidable static, Penzias and Wilson won a Nobel Prize for being the first to discover what is now called, the Cosmic Background Radiation. Their static was an inescapable electromagnetic signal, of very long wavelength, of very low temperature, emanating from every area of space. This exactly satisfied the predictions expected for energy left over from that first burst of ultra-hot pure energy. With this finding, the red shift of visible light that represented the original sign of an expanding universe was seconded by another type of data.

(One need not be trained as a world-class physicist to personally observe the phenomenon of Cosmic Background Radiation. Pick up static on a TV still capable of working through rabbit-ear antennae and a portion of the static that you observe is the electronic signature of the cooled energy left over from God's first light of creation.)

One of the theoretical problems for those troubled by the mechanisms behind the Big Bang is acceptance of the premise that this expanding universe was once so small that its radius literally measured zero units of length. When rolling back the size of this expanding universe, many do not simultaneously roll back the amount of mass contained in space during most of history. As such, the calculated mass density (total mass divided by total area of space) becomes a higher number as space is rolled back. When the volume of space reaches zero, the calculated mass density involves a division by zero, which physicists call a singularity. Many who write popularized summaries of science object to the idea of a singularity as the first stage of the Big Bang and ridicule the idea of the infinite compression of matter. The problem is that these supposed experts are wrong in their assessment of the roll back. Their error results from the failure to properly apply the fundamental math of division by zero.

Physicists often describe a division by zero as infinity, and they mistakenly speak of infinity as though it represents an unattainably large number. This may be a byproduct of the fact that the advanced math of calculus deals with a closely related concept, the infinitesimals. Infinitesimals are conceptual values just a trace larger than zero and are typically called, 'limit zero' (almost zero). When you divide any number by *limit zero*, you get a result that is so huge as to be uncountable. That certainly instills the idea that if you divide by an even smaller value — like true zero - then the result will be an even higher uncountable number. However, that is not really the case. When you divide by true zero, you do not get an even higher number as a result. You get no number at all. Division by zero yields no number that is mathematically defined. Infinity is not a huge number. Infinity is the absence of any number.

When a specific condition in physical science leads to a division by zero, that signifies that this physical state **is undefined** under the conditions that caused the division by zero. By the Lorentz-Fitzgerald correction equations, we know that space, time, and mass are inextricably linked. We also know that any condition that sets the volume of space to zero will also set the corrected values for mass and time to a division by zero. Clearly, when the volume of space is zero, matter is not impossibly compressed. Matter is undefined. You simply cannot roll back space to zero and keep matter as a measurable amount. As such, the starting point for this universe was not impossibly compressed. In the beginning, the universe was mathematically undefined. The beginning was a true state of nothingness, a void without form.

As counterintuitive as this seems, the beginning was not more fanciful or impossible than that which science deals with in real terms every day to make GPS systems work. The Lorentz-Fitzgerald equations work, and they work always, under all conditions. As creatures made of matter, we sense space and time as real constructs and have difficulty sensing a reality in which space and time have meaning only in the presence of matter. However, that is the truth.

The Lorentz-Fitzgerald equations yield a division by zero under certain conditions and those conditions should be understood as reflective of true meaning. That is not the historical viewpoint and that problem continues to plague the popular science of today. Many who write popular science summaries today treat the division by zero as a break down in the laws of physics. Many interpreted the physical division by zero, a singularity, an infinity, as a problem sufficient to reject the big bang model. However, the condition of singularity gained real world confirmation through work published in 1970 by the team of Steven Hawking and Roger Penrose. Their work on black holes proved that singularities were physical realities, and that the origin of this universe from a singularity was physically valid. Opposition to the possibility of singularities could no longer be used to argue against the idea of a universe with a beginning, a beginning that started from nothing.

Hubble and others had shown that our universe had a beginning using evidence of an expanding universe. Penzias and Wilson demonstrated that this universe had a beginning using evidence of the Cosmic Background Radiation. The work of Hawking and Penrose represented the third type of independent evidence demonstrating that this universe did indeed have a beginning. A fourth type of evidence involved the accurate measurement confirming a calculation of the relative prevalence of light-weight chemical elements versus heavy elements in the universe. The truth is that this universe is almost entirely made of the simplest of all atoms, hydrogen, which has a nucleus of only one proton. This preponderance of hydrogen compared to all other elements is most readily explained by a universe which began in a very hot big bang.

These four types of independent confirmatory findings received even more reinforcement as the 20th century matured and lapsed into this century.

As the space age matured beyond the Apollo 11 moon landing, NASA directed significant attention to cosmological research of deep space using sophisticated satellite instruments freed from the interference caused by earth's atmosphere. Two of those projects pursued more detailed measurements of the cosmic background radiation and both have confirmed and extended the findings of Penzias and Wilson.

Launched in 1989 and completing its primary mission in 1994, NASA's COBE satellite (Cosmic Background Explorer) provided extremely precise mapping of the cosmic background radiation. NASA has concluded that these results provide authoritative confirmation of the truth of a big bang beginning for our universe.

Three of the important predictions about the Cosmic Background Radiation were that:

1) it should demonstrate the stretching of wavelength and an extreme amount of cooling as calculated per the current level of universe expansion and age, and that

2) it should be essentially the same energy level regardless of the direction from which it is measured, except that

3) there should be some evidence of very minor differences with slightly higher or lower energy compared to the overall average.

The COBE satellite confirmed it all.

Figures 2 and 3 COBE Satellite Cosmic Radiation Maps [22],[23]

Figures 2 and 3 show the grayscale representation (color in ebook) for two of several color maps summarizing the measurements derived from the COBE satellite. The oval shape of these figures reflects the flattened representation of the globular measurements taken from all directions around Earth. The completely homogenous oval on the left demonstrates the almost perfectly equal distribution of background radiation. This is the measurement achieved with any technique with sensitivity for differences on the order of about 1 part per 100 at temperatures as extreme as about 3 degrees above absolute zero (about negative 270 degrees centigrade). The image on the right represents the grayscale of measurements sensitive to energy differences as slight as 1 part per 10,000. As expected, the background radiation is almost perfectly homogenous throughout the universe. However, with its most sensitive setting, the COBE satellite documented very slight localized peaks of energy exceeding the overall average. This is exactly what one would expect to find for a universe that started out homogenous, but changed to become clumped.

---

[22] https://wmap.gsfc.nasa.gov/resources/cmbimages.html

[23] http://science.nasa.gov/missions/cobe/

Figure 4 WMAP Satellite Final Report [24]

Figure 4 shows the most recent satellite exploration of this primordial energy using the WMAP satellite (Wilkinson Microwave Anisotropy Probe). This satellite has the ability to map differences in energy level as low as 1 part per 10,000 with detailed resolution finer than that achieved by any prior space probe. It confirms and extends the findings of the COBE satellite project.

Among other things, the 2012 Final Report of the WMAP data supports the following conclusions:

1) This universe did have a beginning and the first step in this beginning was light.
2) That beginning was about 13.77 billion current earth years ago.
3) Although space is expanding, the initial appearance of space was not a straight line continuation of the current rate of expansion. Starting from nothing, space began and then dramatically billowed out, growing by a factor of 1 trillion times 1 trillion over a span of time less than one second divided by 1 trillion times 1 trillion.
4) Minor differences in energy density were distributed following a random pattern throughout all areas of this inflating space. These minor differences seeded the clumping of matter into stars and collections of stars seen today.
5) Our directly measurable universe is not all that there is to the total cosmos. All the atoms and measurable energy that fill the four dimensions of our spacetime represent less than 5% of a bigger, grander cosmos.

---

[24] http://map.gsfc.nasa.gov/news/ It is noteworthy that the namesake for this satellite, Dr. David Wilkinson, was the leader of the team of scientists that explained to Penzias and Wilson what their static actually was.

6) Dark matter exists. Dark matter does not generate or absorb electromagnetic radiation of any frequency yet detected. Dark matter interacts with our normal matter only through gravitational effect. In the grand cosmos, dark matter is about 5 times more common than normal matter, representing almost 25% of all that exists in the larger cosmos.

7) Dark energy exists. Dark energy is energy that does not interact with any measuring device made from the typical atoms of our spacetime. Dark energy demonstrates its presence by driving the expansion of this universe at a rate that is not slowing but is getting faster. If we calculated the equivalence of dark energy using an $e=mc^2$ exchange rate, that pool of dark energy would be 14 times more than the sum of everything that we recently thought represented the entire universe. Dark energy represents about 70% of all that defines the full cosmos.

What Does This Mean?

In previous chapters we learned that Einstein's relativity theory established that it is theoretically possible for matter to have been formed by the conversion from energy. In this chapter, we have begun the process of demonstrating that this is exactly what happened.

Faith in God of the ancient Hebrews starts with the belief that life can exist in an immaterial life-form, and that this life-form could be tapped into the ability to control power on a scale of cosmic proportions. Nothing says that this is impossible. Faith continues to build in the face of signs that such a life form truly does exist. Clearly God's possibility is undeniable in the face of modern scientific fact. His actual existence becomes documented through communication with humanity. That faith becomes strong with the recognition that this life form claims credit for creation of all that is seen and unseen and backs that claim through the confirmation of 'dangerous prophesy.' Faith enjoys rock-solid support when we recognize that the scientific record of modernity confirms the details of records established in pre-scientific antiquity. That is exactly what we find today.

Atheism might have once argued against faith in our Creator because of the mistaken belief that the universe could not have been created. However, that and every other atheistic argument are completely debunked today. This universe did have a beginning and the first step in that beginning was the measurable appearance of light. Everything that followed matches the ancient scriptures of Genesis Chapter 1 and simultaneously matches modern science.

The topics described in this chapter represent an example of common ground on which modern science and ancient religion agree. This represents the seed of reconciliation between science and faith. This hasn't happened for several reasons. This reconciliation has been actively derailed by atheists who do not want people to understand the current weakness of the atheist's argument. This reconciliation has also been harmed by well meaning but misguided representatives of faith. As we proceed through the next chapters, I ask all faithful to keep one critical concept in mind. **Truth does not conflict with truth.** This world was created by God, therefore, truthful measurements of this universe can be trusted to reveal the work of God. This is the reality of our modern day condition. Truthful measurements of the way this world works show the direct hand of God. The truth of God's creative process becomes undeniable as we follow the details of what came after the emergence of God's first light.

Chapter 6. The Big Bang and Scripture

Figure 1 Stages of Universe Progression[25]

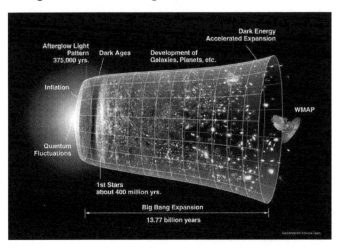

Figure 1 encapsulates the physical changes that have transpired starting with God's first light. The bell shaped structure reflects an initial bursting forth of space from no space followed by a slower continued expansion of space. The fluting of the modern end of the bell shape illustrates that space is currently expanding at a rate that is not slowing but is accelerating. Space is now filled with highly condensed beacons of starlight separated by vast empty spaces. The history of material aggregation reflects a transition from an almost perfectly homogenous origin to a highly clumped modernity. At the extreme modern edge of this diagram, the NASA artist illustrates the presence of the WMAP satellite. This sophisticated tool reflects the intellectual acuity of humanity, a carbon-based life-form capable of self-awareness, curiosity, and intellectual capacity rivaled by no other carbon-based life form in our region of this universe.

---

[25] credit NASA / WMAP Team   https://map.gsfc.nasa.gov

We know that which is summarized in Figure 1 partly because we are able to accurately detect light and measure distance. Because light travels at a fixed velocity, we never really see a distant object in its current state but always in its past state. When we measure light that has traveled from an object 13 billion light years away, we directly observe light that has been traveling toward us for a full 13 billion years. Because of this, we witness the ancient history of our distant universe as directly as any current event within our view.

With the absolute certainty of direct measurement, we know that this universe did indeed have a beginning and that the first step was the emergence of light. We know that space emerged from no prior space. We know that the duration of the sequence between first light and the emergence of mankind was more than six consecutive days. We know that our home planet, Earth, was not one of the first things formed in this universe. Through less direct measurements, we also know that life began in a relatively early step and developed progressively over time. We know that plant life preceded animal life and that animal life in the seas predated that on land. We know that the latest and most advanced form of life to emerge in our region of this universe is the human.

How does this knowledge interface with faith? This knowledge argues against atheism. It also argues against the literalistic view that the creation process was completed in only six consecutive earth days. However, this knowledge does match the portrayal in Genesis Chapter 1 of a creation process involving six general phases. This ancient description of the creation process is told from a perspective that reflects the entire cosmos, not just our home planet.

In this chapter, we explore that which is illustrated in Figure 1. We will summarize the mechanisms that have driven the change from pure light to the modern state of highly condensed balls of fire separated by vast areas of empty space. This review will fulfill the demands of the atheist, Victor Stenger. His 'dangerous prophesy' was recorded 30 centuries before this scientific age and is fully confirmed by scientific measurements today.

We will have the opportunity to recognize documented mistakes and biases of mankind. We will see that these errors do not reflect weakness of the scriptures but actually serve as a recognizable buffer between these ancient scriptures and intentional human meddling. The facts of modern science cannot be claimed to have been contrived by humans intent on self-fulfillment of those ancient scriptures. Indeed, throughout the 20th century, the leadership of the scientific community has been largely antagonistic to those ancient scriptures. Indeed, modern science has dealt a loss to many of the most fervent and sincere of God's faithful. Modern science has dismantled any possible support for the literalistic interpretation of the creation sequence as a short, six-day period. However, in the process of dealing a loss to the minority opinion regarding the interpretation of scripture, modern science established a strong reinforcement of the truths described in the opening chapter of the Bible. The reality is that almost no prior generation has enjoyed a more complete reinforcement of scripture than that afforded to our modern generations. Those who interpret the first chapter of the Bible as a description of six stages of progress unbound by any specific reference of time will recognize that modern science matches ancient scriptures like a key fitted to its lock.

For ease of reference, the full text of Genesis Chapter One and other relevant scriptures have been included into Appendix 1. As introduced in the opening chapter of this book, it is theologically and linguistically correct to interpret the first two verses of Genesis Chapter 1 as an introduction to all that follows. It is correct to read those first two verses as an executive summary, which can be paraphrased as follows:

> IN THE BEGINNING God created the heaven(s) and the earth from a starting point that included no raw materials and no structural framework. That which follows describes how this was done.

That which follows describes a creative process involved six progressive stages, with intervening periods allowing sufficient time for 'percolation' as needed. As covered in the previous chapter, the first of those six progressive steps was the emergence of light, pure energy with no requirement for matter, space or time. The next of those steps deals with the establishment of that which is now translated as 'firmament.' Let us delve into that now.

The Appearance of Matter

This original unfolding of space from no space and the continued expansion of space is typically described by the popular science authors as a mystery beyond all current comprehension. These observations need not be treated as mysterious if we 1) are not biased against the possibility of a creation event and 2) are willing to apply the foundations of relativity theory under all physical conditions including the division by zero. Our best guide to understanding the earliest steps of the birth of our universe is the mathematical foundation encoded into the Lorenz-Fitzgerald correction equations. The foundation supported by these equations gives us the opportunity to explain both the initial inflation and the continuing expansion of space.

In the beginning, this universe was mathematically and physically undefined. Although we are now surrounded by space that extends more than 13 billion light-years in all directions around Earth, the presence of pure energy required no space whatsoever, not even a tiny compressed dot. Upon the emergence of primordial light, space truly was a void, the mathematical and physical result of a Lorentz-Fitzgerald division by zero.

With the precipitation of matter from pure energy according to $e=mc^2$, space and time became mathematically defined. Space burst forth like the unfurling of a parachute. That ultra-fast inflation of space from no space was so rapid that people apply the imperfect analogy of an explosion - a "big bang." That bursting forth of space was precipitous, fast, and hot, but it was not an explosion. An explosion demonstrates a rapid outward expansion from a central point followed by slowing and ultimate cessation of expansion. The expansion of this universe is not an explosion because there is no central point and because the expansion is not stopping. Indeed, after the end of inflation, the rate of the expansion of space has never again demonstrated a period of slowing. Post-inflationary space continues to expand at a rate that increases measurably over time. This is definitely not the behavior of an explosion.

The very rapid inflation of space from nothing is best explained by viewing the appearance of matter like a snowstorm rather than an explosion. At the initiation of the big bang, matter was not being shot outward from a central point of compression but was being formed anew as pure energy transformed into matter according to $e=mc^2$. While pure energy requires no associated space or time, the presence of newly precipitated matter does. The presence of matter simultaneously imposes mathematically defined values for both time and space. From no prior space, space inflated, and the phase transition of pure energy precipitating into matter explains all that needs explaining. The rate of precipitation of new matter driving the secondary appearance of space might have progressed as fast as an explosion, but it occurred in a distributed fashion with no central point of precipitation.

Almost as fast as it began, the emergence of new space stopped and the process of expansion of existing space took over. Some people today are still looking for a force that could explain this sudden termination. That search can stop with application of the most basic concepts of chemical reaction rate kinetics. (No you don't have to be an expert in chemical reaction rate kinetics, but those who are will confirm that I am not speaking gibberish). The termination of the emergence of new space would require no application of outside force because reversible chemical/physical reactions are self-limiting. With the emergence of sufficient reaction product (matter), the reverse process could also take place. Initially, the reaction conditions favored production of matter from an excess of available energy. At some point, the concentration of matter was high enough to allow matter to revert back to energy at an equal rate. When the rate of the reverse reaction (matter > energy) equaled the rate of the forward reaction (energy > matter), then the net formation of new matter would stop, ending the secondary formation of new space from no space. Nothing more exotic than this is needed to explain the self-limited termination of the original inflation of space.

The Clumping of Matter

Even after the termination of the original inflation of space, the volume of space has continued to expand. This expansion is slower than the inflation phase, but it continues and it continues at a rate that always grows faster. Continued expansion would not be a foregone conclusion simply given the precipitation of matter from pure energy. However, the change in the distribution of matter from a very homogenous beginning to a highly clumped modernity provides a mechanism for explaining a continuing expansion of space that gets faster with the passage of additional time.

By the end of the original inflation of space, the vast material content for shaping this universe was spread out evenly, with only very slight local differences in material content. Over time, this changed. The change of the distribution of matter from evenly distributed to highly clumped represents the majority of the history of this physical universe.

The modern distribution of matter is characterized by huge aggregates of gravitationally active mass separated by vast areas of space swept free of matter. Most matter is aggregated into massive stars relatively evenly distributed throughout the scaffolding of space. The size of this collection of stars is worthy of some reflection. Our home planet, along with 7 (or 8) others, orbits a single star, our sun. The gravitational and magnetic forces of this solar system merge to create one complex assembly that has proven hospitable to human life. The area of space taken up by the various orbiting structures of our home solar system is so vast that it took the Voyager 1 space probe more than three decades traveling in excess of 62,000 km/ hr to escape the inner boundary of this single star system. As vast as our home star system is, this represents just one of 100 billion separate star systems in our home galaxy, the Milky Way. Our home galaxy is so vast that these billions of stars are separated by an average distance of five light years. As vast as the Milky Way galaxy is, this is not all this universe holds. In all directions beyond our galaxy lies space expansive enough to hold billions of other galaxies equally as great as our Milky Way.

Overall, the matter that precipitated from that first light of creation has gathered into a collection of more than 25 billion galaxies each with hundreds of billions of individual stars, all separated by about 5 light years of empty space. If we were to estimate the kilowatt-hours of raw energy transformed into enough matter to support this universe we would calculate a number larger than that achieved by

> multiplying 750 billion times a billion, and
> multiplying that result again by a billion times a billion, and
> multiplying that again by a billion times a billion and then --
> multiplying all that times another billion.

As discussed in one of the closing chapters of this book, it is plausible that the formation of our universe was not brought about by an infusion of the vast amount of energy described above. The best current understanding argues that our universe burst forth through an amazing reorganization of nothing to form something with a net energy consumption of zero energy units. Regardless of whether this universe was formed through the infusion of a vast pool of energy, or through the zero-sum control and direction of this vast amount of energy, those of faith have reason to understand that our God truly is an awesome God, a life-force of unrivaled power and might.

Understanding the power behind this universe yields additional reason to understand that it took more than six consecutive earth-days to progress from God's first light to the emergence of the Homo sapiens. The simplest physical evidence of this is the measurable time required to transform the matter precipitated from pure energy into a highly clumped distribution of stars. The average separation of the stars is 5 light years. Nothing less than about 2.5 years would be required to sweep the midpoints of interstellar space free of all matter even if every fleck of matter traveled to its ultimate destination at the speed of light. Now, the early universe was not as large as it is now, but this is more than balanced by the fact that matter travels much slower than the speed of light. The gathering together of solid matter into stars separated by the vast expanses of space took a lot longer than six days. The separation of solid matter into clumps of 'dry land' separated by the 'waters' of deep space took billions and billions of current earth-years. As surely as we know that the sun does not orbit the earth, we know that God's creative processes were not constrained to the duration of six consecutive human days. The days of Genesis are not human days.

Between the blue-green map[26] of the cosmic background radiation and the first documented appearance of visible stars, Figure 1 reflects an interim period called the Dark Ages. This reflects a stage in which matter was so highly energized that it could not even assemble into simple atoms. Just as milk appears opaque due to the scattering of light, this phase of history appears opaque to current measuring devices because light scattering was so intense. We know, by trustworthy measurement, that it took more than 300,000 current earth-years for the frenetic energy of primordial matter to cool sufficiently to allow assembly of electrons, protons and neutrons into simple atoms. It took about 400 million more years for

---

[26] For color, see front cover. Reference:
https://map.gsfc.nasa.gov/media/060915/060915_CMB_Timeline75nt.jpg

those simple atoms to be swept into highly compressed aggregates that became the first generation of stars. It took additional billions of years for those first stars to forge and then release the heavy atoms like carbon and oxygen that represent the essential building blocks for human life. This did not happen in 6 current earth-days!

Data from the COBE and WMAP projects support the description of the early distribution of matter by using the analogy of deep waters. On the sea, wave peaks and troughs form randomly. The probability of a peak at any specific location at any given moment is a purely random number. The WMAP data show very slight differences in the average density of cosmic background radiation. The distribution of very slight differences in energy density are randomly but evenly located throughout space, just as is the case with the distribution of stars today. Like waves upon the seas, these differences reflect pinpoint random variations within a generally homogenous spread. On the sea, larger than average peak waves can form randomly, but gravity acts to pull any specific peak back to the average sea level. Within space, larger than average accumulations of matter formed like a wave, but the dynamics of gravity served to reinforce rather than dissipate the peaks. Within early space, the mutual attraction of matter by other matter would preferentially pull more matter into a forming peak. Through positive reinforcement, areas of above-average matter density emerged as gravitational seeds. Even a slight gravitational advantage would initiate the self-reinforcing accumulation of matter into those zones. Over time, most of space was swept free of material flecks while billions of localized balls of 'solid land' formed.

This mechanism for explaining the aggregation of matter in some places but not others was recognized as a possibility well before the discovery of cosmic background radiation. Indeed, this mechanism had been examined theoretically, complete with preliminary predictions of the types of energy signals that should be detectable if this mechanism was true. All results since the original discovery of cosmic background radiation confirm that this mechanism did indeed play out in God's great universe.

The Clumping of Matter and the Expansion of Space

Earlier in this chapter, I promised that the Lorentz-Fitzgerald equations could demystify both the original appearance and the continued expansion of space. Let us return to a detail that we mentioned to establish the validity of these equations through the incorporation into the engineering of GPS navigation systems. These details will help explain the continued expansion of space. Recall that our GPS satellite systems must correct for time dilation caused by the fast travel of the satellites and by the greater gravitational pull experienced by clocks on the surface of Earth. Gravitational pull, an acceleration force, acts just like high-speed travel. Intense gravitational pull drives a relativistic change in the underlying units for mass, time and length. With high gravitational pull, the units of mass and time are dilated while length is contracted. Stars are collections of mass of such size and density that the gravitational pull can be thousands of times greater than that experienced on Earth. Near these intensely dense centers of gravity, the underlying unit of length would be highly contracted. This morphing of space close to zones of intense gravity has been confirmed through the bending of light rays in the phenomenon called gravitational lensing (Search for information on such structures as the 'Einstein Cross' for additional detail on gravitational lensing.)

So, what happens with the absence of intense gravity experienced in deep space? Here, we would expect the opposite of length contraction. In deep space we would expect the basic unit of length to be expanded compared to that close to the source of intense gravitational pull. With almost no gravitational pull in deep space, length expansion would increase the measurable separation between the galaxies. Since gravity falls proportionally to the distance of separation squared, each increment of length expansion would drive an exponential fall in the gravitational pull in deep space. That is what we see with the expansion of space today. If we would consistently apply the basic rules of physics throughout all conditions of this universe, we need not see universal expansion as a mystery. We need look no further than the Lorentz-Fitzgerald equations to explain it[27].

The Clumping of Matter and the Shaping of Time

Just as the precipitation of matter caused the first definition of the units of space, the appearance of matter caused the first definition of the units of time. In the absence of matter, time was the undefined equivalent of division by zero. Time came into existence because of the persistent emergence of matter transformed from pure energy. Relativity theory teaches us that the underlying value for the unit of time is dependent upon the velocity or gravitational pull of the matter in any region of space. Those characteristics of matter have changed significantly since first light and that means that the underlying value for time has also been changed significantly throughout cosmic history. The original bursting forth of space from no prior space took less than one second of current time. It is equally true that that first second was caused by, and defined by, the universal behavior of matter. The impact of matter on the definition of the underlying units of time continues to this day.

We know the facts summarized in Figure 1 partly because the speed of travel of light is the one feature of this universe that never changes. This means that we can know a lot about the age of the universe because we are very, very good at measuring distance. As surely as we know that Earth orbits the sun, we know that the radius of space around Earth is not less than 13.77 billion light years.

---

[27] The Pioneer spacecrafts launched in the early 1970s have appeared to slow as they left this solar system. A variety of possible explanations have been presented, but I would propose the possibility that the slowing of these spacecrafts is nothing other than a reflection of a literal expansion of the unit of length in deep space.

Therefore, we know that the universe is at least 13.7 billion years old measured in current earth-years.

I specify the age of the universe measured in current earth-years because we know that relativistic changes in the fundamental unit of time play some role in the apparent age of the universe.

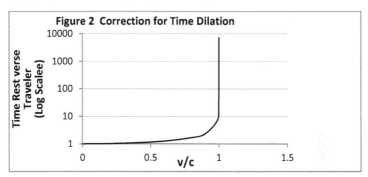

Figure 2 charts the correction for time dilation spanning all values of acceleration from complete rest (v/c=0) through speed of light (v/c=1). In our current state of very slow travel on Earth, the Lorentz-Fitzgerald correction for time expansion would calculate little or no correction for time dilation (v/c=0; bottom left of graph). However, we know that the universe started in the form of pure energy so the Lorentz-Fitzgerald correction for time expansion would calculate an infinite or undefined value for time (v/c=1; top right of graft). Between first light and now, the universe morphed from the original state of undefined time, through periods of greatly expanded time, to our current value for each unit of time. Between these two extremes the units of time changed because the gravitational behavior of matter changed. Between first light and now, the underlying unit for time demonstrated Lorentz-Fitzgerald dilation by more than 10,000-fold for a while, then over 1,000-fold for a while, then 100-fold, 10-fold and every other value ranging between the almost-infinite to Earth's current correction factor of 1.0. I have no calculation for the proportion of history spent at each level along the way but cannot escape the conclusion that the rearrangement of matter over time involved a constant morphing of the underlying unit of time.

Literally, **time changed as times changed**. On the way to the present, the universe aged according to a non-linear scale of time. This means that some of the measured 13.7+ billion years of universal history reflects significant artifact introduced by time dilation. Accounting for non-linear time since the beginning of time means that the universe has not aged a full 13.77 billion current earth-years. Much of that apparent age is a reflection of time dilation during the non-linear process of gravitational arrangement of matter. However, although it is possible that the universe is not a full 13.77 billion current earth-years old, it could not possibly be as young as 10,000 current earth-years. We know this because the universe cannot be younger than the time required for at least one generation of stars to form, age, mature, and explode. That process is measured in the billions of years of current earth-time.

The Formation of Earth

By direct measurement of details that are free from the effects of non-linear time, we know that Earth was not the first structure created and that the interval between first light and the emergence of humankind was not as short as six consecutive earth-days. One method for determining the relative age of Earth versus the universe relies upon direct observation of all phases of the lifecycle of stars coupled with a deep understanding of the periodic table of chemical elements. This is not a difficult task.

One of the first laboratory experiments I conducted as a young student of chemistry involved flame photometry. The elements of Group I and II of the period table (metals like lithium, sodium, and potassium) change the color of a flame when heated. The change in color is unique enough to allow identification of the presence of certain elements in a burning specimen. Other elements absorb light energy of specific frequency with unique patterns supporting an identification method called atomic absorption spectrometry. Even though we cannot reach out and touch any star, we can study the light rays emitted from stars using these and other identification techniques. Based upon that data, we can tell what elements are contained in stars near and far.

We know that almost all matter in this vast universe has become assembled into nothing more complicated than hydrogen, the simplest atomic element with only one proton and one electron. Those billions upon billions of stars that make up the majority of all material content of this universe are made up almost entirely of hydrogen. The next most common element in this universe is helium, which has two protons in its nucleus. Helium can also form by direct assembly of subatomic particles in early space, but that is not the primary source of helium. Helium is primarily formed by the nuclear fusion of hydrogen. Hydrogen can be converted to helium by the squeezing of two single-proton nuclei into one double-proton nucleus. This fusion of two hydrogen nuclei into one helium nucleus releases a tremendous amount of energy. This reaction powers the hydrogen bomb and it is the reaction powering the fires within our sun and all but the oldest stars.

About 98% of all matter in our measurable universe is in the form of hydrogen or helium. However, our planet and all life supported on this planet are made of chemical elements that are much heavier than either hydrogen or helium. Human life requires carbon, oxygen, nitrogen, iron, magnesium, phosphorous and a myriad of other elements that have many more than one or two protons in the nucleus. These heavier elements simply do not form by direct assembly in free space. These elements are formed by the nuclear fusion reactions taking place in very old stars. They become released into the universe only upon the maturation and ultimate explosion of very old stars.

We are able to observe stars across vast distances, and those distant stars demonstrate the condition of stars in the past. We recognize that individual stars do not last forever but follow patterns of formation, aging, and demise much like living creatures. We know that stars are formed from gravitationally compressed clouds of gas. Within these clouds of gas, matter is almost entirely in the form of hydrogen. Once sufficiently compressed, hydrogen nuclei fuse to form helium throughout its period of stable burning.

Earth's sun represents a star in that stable phase of fusing hydrogen as the primary fuel. This means that our sun is a relatively young star (young, but much older than 10,000 years). However, in 5 billion years, the hydrogen supply of our sun will have been consumed to the point that helium and other heavier elements will become consumed as the fuel for continued fusion. In aging stars, helium becomes fused into heavier elements and those heavier elements fuse into still heavier elements. In older stars, fusion involving elements heavier than hydrogen changes the temperature and pressure characteristics in ways that are recognizable. When fusion of elements heavier than hydrogen becomes significant, the density of an aging star reduces, leading to expansion and reddening recognized as a form called "Red Giant." With continued fusion to build still heavier elements, a star density increases leading to a shrinking and hyper-compression. This stage is called "White Dwarf." The dynamics within dwarfs eventually lead to an explosive end to the star. That explosive end to a dying star is called the "Super Nova."

Mankind has directly witnessed all phases of the formation, maturation and explosive death of stars and we can measure the relative proportion of chemical elements at each stage by studying the details of the wavelengths of light given off by any given star. We are certain that the content of the heavier chemical elements found on Earth increases as a star progresses through the aging process. The heaviest and rarest of the elements found on Earth are formed only in the very latest stages immediately preceding the explosive death of an aged star.

With no significant risk of reversal by future findings, we can say that planet Earth could not possibly have been formed on the first day of creation, because planet Earth is formed from elements that were released into nature only through the formation, maturation, aging and explosive death of at least one generation of stars. This is completely consistent with other measurements that indicate that the universe is more than 13 billion years old while our sun is only a little less than half of that age.

The Sun-Earth-Moon System

While the first stars of this universe formed around 13 billion years ago, our sun is only about 5 to 6 billion years old. Our home planet is slightly younger that its sun, with an age around 4.5 billion years. The moon for our planet is even younger, formed almost 100 million years after the origin of our planet.

Our solar system started as a cloud of hydrogen gas and interstellar dust just as have all other stars. This type of gas cloud, or nebula, has been viewed by the Hubble telescope. One of the more massive nebulae viewed by the Hubble is named, "Pillars of Creation."[28] Starting with the gravitational compression of a nebula, stars are 'born' and begin the certain progression toward the aged supernova.

The explosion of an aged supernova relatively near our current location provided the raw materials for 8 planets (9 counting Pluto), more than 140 moons, and countless asteroids and comets now orbiting in this solar system. The forces released by that supernova explosion triggered an imbalance in the gravitational compression within that local cloud of gases, initiating gravitational self-compression within the nebula. Ultimately, that self-compressed

---

[28] Seek any of the many ESA/Hubble images such as
https://cdn.spacetelescope.org/archives/images/publicationjpg/heic1501a.jpg

cloud of gas and dust achieved pressures sufficient to ignite hydrogen fusion within an interstellar body that is now our Sun.

The building up of planet Earth and the 7 (or 8) others that orbit our Sun involved the continued, successive collision and merger of smaller objects like the adding of clay to an emerging sculpture. The highly cratered appearance of Earth's moon provides evidence that the past included a lot of violent smashing and bashing. Matter became swept about in a gravitational tug of war carried out throughout the solar system. In 1994, mankind had sufficient technology to observe several interstellar collisions in real time. In that year, the huge comet named Shoemaker-Levy 9 impacted the planet Jupiter. Before impact, the comet broke into several large fragments providing the opportunity to directly observe multiple explosive impacts on this neighboring planet. Closer to home, the widespread availability of dash-cams used in Russia in 2013 provided dramatic recordings of the slamming of a moderately sized meteor into Earth's atmosphere. Direct measurements such as these confirm the process of gravitational clumping of matter. These and other processes help us understand that gravitational processes did indeed lead to the building up of Earth through the accumulation of smaller clumps that have smashed together. Indeed, isotopic studies of Earth's water suggest that much of the H_2O for this planet is older than the assembled planet (the amount of deuterium, aka heavy hydrogen with an extra neutron, is less than expected for the age of this planet). That means that a significant portion of Earth's water was formed elsewhere and gravitationally captured during a period of intense interstellar bombardment.

Today, the intensity of interstellar 'bumper clump' is less than it was in the past. The arrangement of the planets, moons, asteroids and comets have stabilized. Today's Sun-Earth-Moon system can be truthfully described as a stable clockwork mechanism, even though the timing of each element relative to the other seems imperfectly synchronized on the scale of single days or months within a single year. However, this rare celestial system, with one great light for day and one lesser light for night is perfectly synchronized to optimize an annual pattern of seasonal change.

In a uniquely advantageous manner, the angle of the axis of Earth's rotation is tilted relative to the sun and the angle of this tilt happens to approximate one-half of 45 degrees. The tilt of that angle demonstrates a unique reversal halfway through each annual orbit around the sun. This fortunate arrangement is coupled with the uniquely advantageous assumption of an almost perfectly circular orbit of Earth around the sun. While the shape of the orbit of almost any object around another object typically follows the shape of an ellipse, Earth enjoys a circular annual orbit. Earth is spared the effects of either exaggerated closeness or exaggerated distance from its sun. Combine all of these unique elements and you have a clockwork optimized for distributing moderate seasonal changes across the broadest possible range for both northern and southern hemispheres. Earth's moon, that lesser light of the night, is not a bystander but is a critical, active participant in the control of seasonal change. Without the gravitational balance introduced by the orbit of the moon around the earth, the cycle of Earth's annual tilting would break into a chaotic mess, ending the moderate seasonal change that is critical for life.

Although the orbits of the moon around the earth and of the earth around the sun are perfectly moderated for the support of life on this planet, this system did not begin as an orderly system. The moon is a late addition to this solar system, formed as a rearrangement step about 100 million years after the initial formation of the earth. One of the ways we know this is that we can measure the moon actually moving away from Earth rather than toward it. Also, the moon's chemical footprint closely matches that of Earth's outer crust. For these two reasons, the moon is thought to have formed when a portion of Earth budded off to form a separate body. One might debate the details of how this came about, but it is clear that our moon represents an example of ejecta, thrown off from Earth, not debris captured from a distance.

The most commonly held view is that our moon formed as the result of a powerful, off-center collision between Earth and another interstellar object.[29] The impacting object was about half as large as our emerging planet was at the time of collision (it was about the size of Mars). This collision was so powerful that it produced a merging of both objects, significantly increasing the total mass of planet Earth. However, like a big rock dropped into a deep puddle of mud, that collision caused a rebound splash. A glob of Earth's crust was ejected upon impact and that glob achieved a unique orbit around Earth, one that is gradually moving outward. Suspended in space, this glob of ejected earth-crust was large enough to demonstrate gravitational self-compression. However, that self-compression did not form a perfect sphere. The moon is lopsided, slightly pear shaped, with one hemisphere heavier than the other. The moon would tend to rotate independently of its period of orbit except that its heavy side is trapped in a downward orientation relative to Earth's pull.[30]

The Origin of Life

Life exists and there is not an atheist alive who can tell you why or how life came to be. Atheists cannot tell you how life came to be except with adamant rejection of the possibility that God had a hand in it. A central tenant of both Judaism and Christianity is that life is an attribute of God, shared as a gift from God.

"God or No God," that is the real question. That is the dichotomy of the ages. Both atheists and the faithful frequently act as though Darwin's theory of evolution is the pivot point upon which that

---

[29] Very recent modifications of theory suggest that more than one smaller impact released more than one smaller portions of ejecta, but the net result of the process remains the same.

[30] The reader might enjoy searching for any number of video demonstrations of the "libration of the moon" which represents monthly swinging of the moon like a pendulum. If it could, the moon would rotate independently of its Earth orbit.

dichotomy is resolved. Neither side could be more incorrect in their assessment of the importance of Darwin's theory of evolution. No aspect of science is so poorly taught while also being so easy to understand. Both the atheistic community and the faithful are to blame.

Those who rely upon the theory of evolution as the alternative to the creation of life by God must admit that the theory of evolution says absolutely nothing about how life started. The theory of evolution presents no fact that refutes belief in God as the one and only source of life. Every believer in God as our creator should understand that Darwin's observations about the mechanisms for the emergence of biological diversity casts no aspersion against the reality of our Creator. The antagonism against evolution within the community of believers is derived from incorrect insistence that Genesis Chapter 1 speaks literally of six consecutive days. For reasons already addressed, that interpretation is as verifiably wrong as was the medieval belief that the sun orbits the earth.

The theory of evolution is based solely upon the recognition of the repeated use of common structures not significantly different from what one would see if they studied the development of computers, or airplanes, or any other construct that has progressed from simple to complex. This feature of biological observation only addresses mechanisms for change, not origin, and it says absolutely nothing that rules out the possibility of God. Darwin's observations describe how a relatively small set of primordial life forms could evolve to a more diverse set of related forms and functions. Darwin originally proposed this theory in the mid 19th century when science mistakenly taught that a creation event was not possible. Based upon that error, many assumed that the absence of God is inextricably linked to Darwin's teachings. That is simply not true. Many believed that details for an origin of life without God would be discovered by future developments. However, that 19th century expectation has never been realized. Well into the 21st century,

Darwin's fans cannot generate life from that which is not alive and cannot restore life once life is lost.

Those of faith recognize that life cannot be generated or restored because life is not a mechanistic byproduct of the organization of matter. Life is an attribute of the immaterial Creator, shared directly by and received from that Creator. Just as is the case for the Creator, the force of life itself is immaterial. This, of course, represents nothing more than my declaration of faith, but it is not without reason. The first chapter of the Bible teaches that life originated in a progressive sequence. That sequence has been confirmed by modern science giving reason to believe those old scriptures.

Science cannot describe how life began but has documented a sequential appearance of various forms of plant and animal life. Humans represented the final major stage of development in the emergence and diversification of life forms. Humans were preceded by lower level animal life, which was preceded by plant life. Terrestrial life was preceded by the initial development of life within the seas. This scientific ordering of the origin of life matches that recorded 3000 years before the age of Darwin. This is an example of the confirmation of ancient prophesy that could not possibly be the result of human self-fulfillment.

A Just Right Universe

Dr. Hugh Ross is among a set of authors teaching excellent popularized summaries of the astounding set of extraordinarily precise features of nature that cause Earth to be a perfect environment for life.[31] A small subset of these fortunate advantages include placement into orbit of a perfect collection of raw materials at the perfect distance from a perfect star. Our sun needed to be a

---

[31] Ross, Hugh. "Chapter 14. A 'Just Right' Universe." The Creator and the Cosmos; How the Greatest Scientific Discovery of the Century Reveals the Existence of God. Colorado Springs, USA: NavPress Group, 1994. 105-21. Print 3rd.

type of star that was stable enough to avoid an early explosion. It needed to be large enough to gravitationally capture and hold a cohesive system of the mass spewed forth from a neighboring supernova explosion. Of all the non-burning raw materials that ultimately clumped together to form planets orbiting our sun, our planet, Earth, enjoys the advantage of being made of the perfect blend of raw materials to form a rocky planet with an optimal gravitational mass, with a hot central core capable of generating a magnetic field, orbiting the sun at a perfect distance, in a perfectly circular orbit. Our planet is structured and positioned just perfectly to enjoy a temperate planetary crust complete with water in liquid phase. Earth enjoys an abundance of biologically compatible elements held in a perfect blend of solid, liquid and gaseous phases in close proximity to that water. Our planet demonstrates magnetic polarization, which is a fortunate attribute not universally shared by every planetary structure. This magnetic polarization provides fortunate navigational assistance utilized by natural sensors of many animals, or through simple machines made by mankind but it also serves a life-saving role beyond navigational convenience. Acting like the advanced edge of airplane's wing, Earth's magnetic field serves as an insulator against harmful interstellar radiation. This magnetic shield causes the majority of toxic cosmic radiation to flow around and past Earth. The gaseous atmosphere of this planet supports respiration of land-based life, but this gaseous wrapping of our planet provides another protective shield much like that of the magnetic shell. While literally "light as air," our atmosphere is sufficiently non-compressible to protect Earth's crust from physical impact from space debris. Friction against our atmosphere causes almost all meteors falling to Earth to burn completely before striking a damaging blow. Protection against life-changing bombardment from space has not been absolute. Earth has been the target of some impacts that had profound impact on life. To this point, all life-changing impacts have been supportive of the life of Homo sapiens.

I would refer to the works of Dr. Ross and others[32,33,34] for additional detail regarding the precise tuning required to allow this universe to support life. The scientific truth is that precise tuning of multiple physical constants and other attributes have been confirmed. Without this fine-tuning, you would not live on this planet.

What Does This Mean?

What this means is that the Genesis Chapter 1 is literally true, when you don't take the wrong word literally. Faith in God of the ancient Hebrews is a reasonable prospect because the ancient scriptures of the Hebrews reflect a trustworthy *a priori* summary of the work of our Creator.

At a minimum, the facts summarized to this point mean that God remains possible even in this highly scientific age. The only data-driven scientific argument in support of atheism is more than 100 years out of date. During the 20th and 21st centuries science has continually added to a pattern of evidence fully concordant with mainstream professions of faith. In truth, modern science reveals that God is more than possible. **God is scientifically plausible.**

The atheist, Victor Stenger, argued that faith in biblical scripture should involve reference to a biblical prophesy that could never be explained by intentional human self-fulfillment. I could argue that this is not a valid requirement, or that the atheistic rejection of fulfilled prophesy has been unreasonable. However, the truth is that Genesis Chapter 1 stands up perfectly to Stenger's challenge. I will not argue that Stenger's challenge is unreasonable. I argue that Stenger's challenge has been fully satisfied through the complete

---

[32] Davies, Paul. The Mind of God: The Scientific Basis for a Rational World. New York, Touchstone, 1993. ISBN 0671687875

[33] Greene Brian R. The Elegant Universe: Superstrings, Hidden Dimensions, and the Quest for the Ultimate Theory, W.W. Norton & Company, Inc., New York, 1999. ISBN 0-393-04688-5

[34] Schroeder, Gerald L. The Science of God: The Convergence of Scientific and Biblical Wisdom. New York, Free Press, 2009 ISBN 9781439129586

match between the 3000-year old scriptures of Genesis Chapter 1 and the facts of modern science.

It is worthwhile to return to that summary of scripture versus science introduced in an opening chapter of this book.

Executive Summary of Genesis Chapter 1

IN THE BEGINNING… God created the heavens and earth. The starting point was the absence of anything. This is an introductory statement applicable to all steps that follow. This is not a description of the first step per se.

There was indeed a beginning; this universe has not existed forever. The starting point held no matter, no time, and no space. Planet Earth was not formed as a first step; Earth was a late addition to the universe.

The First Day (Age)

"Let there be Light" was the first creative step.

Light, intensely hot electromagnetic radiation (EMR), was the first step of the origin of the universe.

The Second Day (Age)

After the creation of light and before the emergence of life of any type, firmament (the sky), was formed. As per Psalms 104, the heavens were spread out like a tent. Into the firmament the lights of the sky were placed.

The scaffolding of space burst into existence from no prior space like the opening of a parachute. Precipitation of matter from pure energy according to $e=mc^2$ directly caused this. Stars formed as the earliest and still predominant structures in space.

The Emergence of Life, on Multiple Days (Ages). 3, 5 and 6[35]

The emergence of life proceeded with plant life first and humans last. Animal life in the sea preceded animal life on land. Plant life originated on 'Day 3', animal life on 'Day 5' and Humans on 'Day 6'.

The known pattern of the emergence of life matches the ancient declaration that plants preceded animals and sea animals preceded land animals. Humans were last.

The Fourth Day (Age)

Between the emergence of plant life and the emergence of animal life, additional attention is directed to Earth and its two great lights yielding a time–compliant system, marking the passage of seasons, days and years.

The Sun-Earth-Moon system was a late addition to the universe. The final adjustment and control of the earth's rotational axis by the moon completed a finely tuned clockwork mechanism that optimally distributes seasonality across the earth.

The Sixth and Final Step – The Dawn of Humanity

Humans were the last of all animals to be created and differed from all other animals through the unique gift of a soul / mind that was created as an image of God. The human soul / mind is a reflection of the creative, thinking Being who conceived and constructed this universe.

Humans demonstrated the most recent emergence of any species of animal. Nodal branching of the higher branches of the 'tree of life' has not continued after the emergence of the human. No

---

[35] The emergence of animal life addressed on the 5th day of Genesis is not summarized as a separate step but is thought best summarized together with all three steps, (3, 5 and 6, that address emergence one or more forms of life.

other animal rivals the creative drive and capacity of the human mind.

Even a skeptic must admit that these ancient scriptures correctly revealed truths that would not be known to humanity until these modern days. The opening chapter of the Bible accurately presaged our modern scientific knowledge. There was a beginning. Light was the first step, followed by the unfurling of space and formation of stars, with formation and precise arrangement of our solar system following as a late modification. The emergence of life was laid out in the correct order long before mankind could possibly know that there even was an orderly emergence of life. Life originated with plants preceding animals. Animal life within the seas was correctly described as preceding animal life on land. Humanity was correctly described as the last of all animal life to appear.

One could not ask for a better match between the Bible and modern science. However, the match between science and scripture gets even stronger when the details of the Sun-Earth-Moon system are closely considered. Overly literalistic interpretation of scripture professes that planet Earth was instantly formed on Day 1, had sprouted all plant life including trees and shrubs with seeded fruit on Day 3, but had no sun or moon until Day 4. That literalistic interpretation is a favorite target of atheistic attack, but that represents a very lame, straw dog argument. The truth is that these ancient scriptures attended to detail regarding the Sun-Earth-Moon system in exactly the correct order. Attention to the Sun-Earth-Moon system on the 4th day reflects detailed knowledge that would absolutely remain out of reach of any human until the last half of the 20th century. The ancients said that God taught that attention to the Sun-Earth-Moon system reflected the fourth step of creation. That is exactly what modern science has uncovered. Stenger's demand has been nailed!

So, tell me if you can, how does the advanced understanding of the origin of Earth and our solar system support atheism? The truth is that nothing related to the science of the 20th century argues against the possibility of God. The more a person understands about science, the more one sees the truth. Science does not argue against God. Modern science actually refutes atheism. Modern science refutes atheism and that is why the atheistic leadership of modern science has not done a better job of educating the public on these topics.

To ensure that I have not missed something, I refer you to important summaries of modern science written by other authors. Study these references [36] [37] [38] [39] and continue to study those who reference them. Some of these references reflect passive support for atheism. In previous chapters I have referred you to specific references presenting explicit arguments for atheism. Study them all and use your best sense of reason and logic. Ask what fact I have omitted from my defense of faith and you will find that I have not omitted any fact that scientifically argues against the plausibility of God. You will find an inescapable truth. Atheism is not based upon modern science. Atheism is debunked by modern science.

We will discuss in a later chapter why the average person continues to hear that science argues against God when that is not the truth. For now, it is best to complete the full discussion of the scientific ramifications of the Lorentz-Fitzgerald equations and Einstein's theory of relativity as understood around the 100th year anniversary of Einstein's work. Then we can move onto other topics.

---

[36] Hawking, Stephen. The Illustrated **A Brief History of Time**, Updated and Expanded Edition, Bantam Dell, New York, 1996.

[37] Hawking, Stephen. The Universe in a Nutshell, Updated and Expanded Edition, Bantam Dell, New York, 2001.   Combined editions ISBN: 9780307291172

[38] Davies, Paul. Other Worlds. Space, Superspace and the Quantum Universe. Simon and Schuster, New York, 1980 (1982). ISBN 0671422278

[39] Greene Brian R. The Elegant Universe: Superstrings, Hidden Dimensions, and the Quest for the Ultimate Theory, W.W. Norton & Company, Inc., New York, 1999

Chapter 7. Realms Beyond This Spacetime?

Previous chapters have addressed that which is known. This chapter introduces that which is possible. We will look at those details of modern science that point to the existence of dimensions beyond our 4-dimensional spacetime. We will find that the cutting edge of science screams for recognition of the presence of additional realms of spacetime beyond our own. Cutting edge science is fully consistent with the idea of heaven.

Today we know of a type of matter called dark matter and a type of energy called dark energy. Dark matter is called 'dark' because it is invisible to most of our physical and chemical detectors. This is because dark matter does not radiate, reflect or absorb light of any frequency that we recognize. Dark matter makes its presence known only through gravitational interaction with matter in our world. First discussed in 1930, dark matter remains unexplained today. Common popularized descriptions continue to expound upon the mysterious nature of this dark matter. It need not be treated as such a mystery.

Dark energy and dark matter remain mysterious largely because the atheistic leadership of modern science remains antagonistic to any idea that reinforces religious faith. They reject the possibility of intelligent life existing in immaterial form. They reject the idea of heaven. They reject the idea of resurrection of the body, a body remade in a way that is never again subject to death. The faithful of this highly scientific age have every reason to embrace the idea that 'a higher power' could be more than a poetic concept. We have every reason to believe that God, heaven, and resurrection of the body are possible under a cosmic structure that includes a type of light unconstrained by the upper limit of Einstein's light speed.

Light Divided

Current scientific leadership has been unwilling to challenge Einstein's declaration that nothing can travel faster than the speed of light. However, calculation of the Lorentz-Fitzgerald correction equations using actual velocity faster than the speed of our light reveals a mechanism that could readily explain solid matter that appears dark from our perspective. An additional realm of material existence could exist – literally in our midst – but we would be physically blind to its presence. Blindness can be real, but blindness to an object does not render that object less than real. This truism helps us approach the topic of dark matter.

We use the term 'dark matter' to describe a construct of nature that is measurable only through gravitational activity. Let me propose that this is fully consistent with ancient Hebrew Scriptures. The only real difference is that modern science has used the adjective 'dark' in the opposite perspective relative to that taught by Genesis 1.

As brilliant as the light of our current spacetime might seem, let me propose that our mortal realm is the product of a type of energy that is less powerful, darker, than another class of energy. Specifically, let me suggest that the first step of creation involved the creation of light followed without delay by division into two distinct types separated as completely as night versus day. The Lorentz-Fitzgerald equations teach us that such a separation is physically achievable through a key difference in relative transmission velocity. These equations teach us that c, the speed of Einstein's light could represent a boundary between darkness (slower transmission speed) and heavenly light (faster transmission speed). While Einstein rejected any notion of transmission faster than the speed of light, this rejection is questionable.

Genesis Chapter 1 and Job 38

The scriptural basis for receptivity to additional realm(s) of existence based upon a distinction between two different types of light originates in the earliest verses of Genesis Chapter 1 and in the Book of Job. The Genesis verses that describe the first phase of creation are reproduced below.

1:3 And God said: 'Let there be light' And there was light.

1:4 And God saw the light, that it was good; **and God divided the light from the darkness.**

1:5 And God called the light Day, and the darkness He called Night And there was evening and there was morning, one day.

It has always struck me as odd that scripture would attend to such an obvious detail as 'God divided the light from the darkness.' If darkness is the absence of light, then it appears unnecessary to explicitly divide light from darkness. Why was this division important enough to earn a place in the fourth verse of God's self-introduction to His creatures? Could this be more than a poetic device? To help us explore these questions, let me pose another question, one that is not of my design.

Tell me, if you know all: Which is the way to the dwelling place of light, and where is the abode of darkness? Job 38:19

This admonition from God to those who think they are smart sets the stage for expecting separate realms of existence for good versus evil. Additional scripture, drawn from the New Testament helps complete the faith-based expectation of additional realms of existence beyond this spacetime. Christians of all denominations understand that Christ declared that His Kingdom is not of this world.

Jesus answered, "**My kingdom does not belong to this world**. John 18:36

To the contrary, Christ has said that this mortal world is ruled by Satan, the prince of darkness.

And now I have told you before it come to pass, that, when it is come to pass, you might believe. Hereafter I will not talk much with you: **for the prince of this world cometh, and has nothing in me**. John 14:29-30

The Biblical contrast between light and darkness consistently symbolizes a conflict between good and evil. Could it be that the distinction is not merely poetic? Could the separation of the dwelling place of the light from the abode of darkness have been brought into effect through the division of light into two types as in Genesis 1:4? Let me propose that the separation of light described in Genesis 1:4 does not deal with the trivial distinction between noon and midnight in Jerusalem. Let me propose that this verse deals with God's purposeful separation of evil from good at the very first step of the creation of this world.

For those of faith, let me get a little ahead of myself. Mankind was not destined for entrapment in this mortal realm, the "abode of darkness." We were destined for a paradise at least partially removed from this realm. We were destined for a very real place within the "dwelling place of light." By virtue of our physical birth into this place, we must now find a way out. In truth, there is a way and that way is the spoken of as 'the Light.' We will end this book with a more complete discussion of that topic. For now, we will examine how the realities of modern science set the stage for a better understanding of these scriptural teachings.

The Fitzgerald Ratio and the Square Root of Negative One

The Lorentz-Fitzgerald corrections that calculate the highly malleable units of time, length and mass, have been proven through real-world application. Let us review all three correction equations below.

Chapter 4, Equation 1 Lorentz-Fitzgerald Correction for Time

$$t' = \left(\frac{t}{\sqrt{1 - \frac{v^2}{c^2}}} \right)$$

Chapter 4, Equation 2 Lorentz-Fitzgerald Correction for Mass

$$m' = \left(\frac{m}{\sqrt{1 - \frac{v^2}{c^2}}} \right)$$

Chapter 4 Equation 3 Lorentz-Fitzgerald Correction for Length

$$l' = \left(l * \sqrt{1 - \frac{v^2}{c^2}} \right)$$

In these equations

t = time at rest, and t' = corrected time;
m = mass at rest, and m' = corrected mass;
l = length at rest and l' = corrected length;
v = actual speed and
c = speed of light in a vacuum.

Critical to each correction equation is the Fitzgerald ratio that involves the calculation of the square root of a value.

$$\left(\sqrt{1 - \frac{v^2}{c^2}} \right)$$ **The Fitzgerald Ratio**

The result of each correction is driven by a square root value involving the ratio of actual velocity divided by the speed of Einstein's light. That value taken to its square root is not simply the squared ratio of velocities but is 1 minus that squared ratio. Based upon that, is it clear why actual velocity (v) greater than the speed of light (c) bothered Einstein? Einstein rejected any possibility of velocities faster than the speed of light because that would cause the Fitzgerald ratio to yield a result as the square root of a negative number.

Step-by-step processing of that calculation goes like this:

1. Faster than light travel causes the ratio of $\frac{v^2}{c^2}$ to assume a value greater than 1.
2. That ratio is subtracted from 1 yielding a negative number.
3. Calculation of the square root of that negative number is required to solve the correction equation for either time, mass, or length.

The problem with that answer is that **square roots of negative numbers do not exist in the set of real numbers.** It simply is not possible to multiply any real number by itself and end up with a negative number as the result.

Einstein was daring enough to completely revise the understanding of the conservation laws. He was adventurous enough to rewrite the literal definitions of time and space. He was bold enough to accept credit – in his lifetime – as the greatest physicist since Sir Isaac Newton. However, Einstein was not bold enough to accept the possibility that real-world problems could ever involve answers that are not members of set of real numbers. As such, he completely rejected any possibility of travel faster than the speed of light. For Einstein, rejection of faster-than-light travel was not simply an end-result of his relativity theory. Rejection of faster-than-light travel was a fundamental concept, a starting point from which other fruits of relativity theory were conceived.

In 1966, when writing his popularized text, _Understanding Physics_, [40] Isaac Asimov did not overtly challenge Einstein's conclusion, but he was not fundamentally disturbed by the fact that faster-than-light travel would cause the corrected values of time, mass, and length to calculate as the square root of a negative number. Unlike Einstein, Asimov did not absolutely reject the possibility of faster-than-light travel, but he understood that such a result would not be directly measurable in our real-world setting. However, Asimov left open for consideration the possibility that 'not measurable' in our real-world setting is not the same as 'not true.'

Since his publication of the special theory of relativity in 1905, Einstein's conclusion that nothing travels faster than light has been unquestionable by most serious scientists. Since that time, explicit suggestions of faster-than-light travel have occasionally been raised

---

[40] Isaac Asimov, Volume II, Chapter 7. Understanding Physics, Original © 1966, reprinted by Barnes and Noble Books, New York, 1993 ISBN 0880292512

for consideration, but have been treated as the meaningless musings of science fiction writers, blissful ignorance, the folly of idiots, or errors in laboratory measurement. However, in recent years, the prospect of faster-than-light signal transduction has received serious consideration by reputable research groups. Cautious receptivity to the possibility of superluminal travel has gained traction because the 20th century ended with additional physical findings that were not yet perceived when Einstein first published his theory of special relativity in 1905.

After Einstein's general theory of relativity was published, technical developments showing real-world application of square roots of negative numbers started to flourish in the sciences of aerodynamics and electronics. In addition, the period after Einstein's publications gave rise to mathematical examination of Einstein's equations. That work gave reason to expect that the universe was expanding (now confirmed) and that the complete cosmos contained at least one additional dimension of spacetime. Today, there is every reason to examine the possibility that this expanding universe does, indeed, represent only a subset of all dimensions of space. There is good reason to recognize that the Lorentz-Fitzgerald calculations point to a plausible mechanism for locating those extra dimensions.

Imaginary Numbers in the 20th Century

Two centuries before Einstein's day, square roots of negative numbers were named 'imaginary numbers' because these values appeared to hold no importance in this physical world. When Einstein first published his theory of relativity, imaginary numbers were mathematical oddities of interest only to pure mathematicians. Euler's identity is a mathematical relationship involving multiplication and exponentiation of a mixture of imaginary numbers with real numbers that gives an unexpected real-number result. Math fans appreciate this relationship as an example of natural beauty, but no one can say for sure that they know what it means. Let me provide some background.

Leonhard Euler (pronounced Oiler) was an 18th century mathematical genius. One of the contributions for which Euler is most well-known involves the mathematics of natural exponential growth (like population growth and compound interest). Natural exponential growth follows a logarithmic pattern that was not in base 10. Euler determined that this pattern followed logarithmic growth in a base of approximately 2.718. Like π, this logarithmic base is an irrational number, 2.71828... continuing through a limitless number of decimal places without end and without repetition. It is one of the most special numbers in arithmetic and today is simply abbreviated as 'e.'

In his studies of 'e,' Euler discovered something about the interaction between e, π, and the square root of negative 1 that is still hard to explain today. When the square root of negative 1 is multiplied by any non-zero number, the result is typically an imaginary number, not a real number. However, Euler found that **π** and **e** (non-zero real numbers) interact with the square root of negative 1 (the fundamental imaginary number) in one multiplication pattern that yields a real number result!

$$e^{\pi * \sqrt{-1}} = -1 \qquad \text{Euler's Identity, Direct Form}$$

This can be rearranged to show zero as the result.

$$e^{\pi * \sqrt{-1}} + 1 = 0 \qquad \text{Euler's Identity, Common Form}$$

This equation shows the four most unique real numbers (0, 1, e, and π) interacting with the fundamental counting unit of the imaginary numbers ($\sqrt{-1}$) to yield an unexpected real number result.

No one has claimed to know all that this relationship means. At the very least, Euler's identity demonstrates that the set of real numbers and the set of imaginary numbers are not completely distinct. Based upon Euler's identity, we should expect that the real numbers and imaginary numbers share a real-world intersection at the value of zero. Indeed, the modern use of complex numbers relies upon that assumption.

Square roots of negative numbers were originally of interest only to pure mathematicians like Euler. Today, however, these numbers have found practical use in the modern applied sciences. Today the imaginary numbers are viewed as a fully valid set of numbers separate from, but complementary to, the set of real numbers. The imaginary numbers have completely valid mathematical properties supporting addition, subtraction, multiplication, and division just as with the set of real numbers. Those rules for mathematical operations with imaginary numbers are not always as simple as the rules for operations with real numbers but they are systematic, valid rules of math.

The set of "imaginary numbers" are not part of the set of "real numbers", but they *really are numbers.* By way of analogy, two separate sets of numbers can be compared to two separate languages. Consider the American-English language printed in Calibri 11 point font compared to the ancient Egyptian language scribed in hieroglyph. Which of these is the real language? I can read one language and not the other but that does not mean that the language I cannot read is less valid. Both are real languages. In that same way, both real numbers and imaginary numbers demonstrate complete mathematical validity.

Practical use of imaginary numbers works like this. Any imaginary number can be defined by taking any conceivable value from within the set of real numbers and multiplying that number by the square root of negative 1 (abbreviated as i). Using imaginary numbers, the square root of negative 9 can be valued as $3i$ (the real number 3, times i, the square root of negative 1). This pattern can be applied to all real numbers so the set of imaginary numbers includes a complementary value for every value within the countless set of real numbers.

$$\sqrt{-9} = 3i \text{ which is } +3 \times \sqrt{-1}$$

$$\sqrt{-25} = 5i \text{ which is } +5 \times \sqrt{-1}$$

Etc.

Just like real numbers can enumerate a relative position along a number line, the imaginary numbers can serve as valid enumerators of relative position along a number line. The number line for the imaginary numbers is not the same as that for real numbers, but the relative position of positive and negative values for the set of imaginary numbers works exactly like that for number line of real numbers.

Figure 1 illustrates the concept of imaginary and real numbers as two valid number lines operating in different dimensions but intersecting at zero. This demonstrates visually that the set of imaginary numbers is not less suitable than the set of real numbers as a system for enumeration of relative placement on a separate number line.

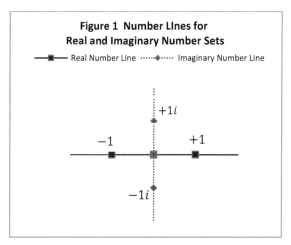

The Russian mathematician, Nikolai Joukowski (1847-1921), was one of the first to find practical utility for the imaginary numbers in the form of complex numbers. Complex numbers provide real world benefit by making use of the two dimensions reflected in Figure 1 above. Complex numbers reflect one dimension of value as a real part and a second dimension of value as the imaginary part. Following the construct represented in Figure 1, graphs of complex numbers can be drawn with the real number portion reflecting the horizontal placement (X-axis point) and the imaginary dimension reflecting the vertical placement (Y-axis point).

Joukowski was exploring various behaviors of imaginary numbers through an exercise in pure math. Starting with a simple circle on 2-dimensional graphs like Figure 1, Joukowski treated the coordinates of the circle as though they reflected complex numbers (y coordinate as imaginary and x coordinate as real). He subjected these complex numbers to various mathematical manipulations, just to see what happened. One of his exercises calculated a value derived by adding the reciprocal of a coordinate point to the original coordinate value and replotting the results on the same X, Y graph. We won't struggle through the details of that math except to reveal the outcome. Starting with a circle, Joukowski's calculations yielded new coordinates shaped as an aerodynamically functional wing!

'Joukowski transform equations' quickly became a fundamental tool for sophisticated aerodynamic engineering. As the 20th century progressed, aeronautic engineers used variations of the starting circle(s) and transformation equations to create experimental profiles for wings. Each shape would yield different characteristics of lift and drag so variations on the technique could be used to optimize wing profiles for different uses. This practical engineering process demonstrates one of the first real-world uses for imaginary numbers in the form of complex numbers – numbers that are part real, part imaginary.

Electronic engineering and quantum mechanics represent two other fields in which imaginary numbers commonly afford a practical solution to real-world problems. Complex numbers (imaginary part and real part) provide a system for solving problems involving simultaneous change in two different but related characteristics of some real world event. A common example is the measurement of resistance in electrical circuits powered using alternating current. When dealing with direct current, it is a simple process to measure resistance across a circuit using simple real numbers. With alternating current (AC), both the direction and amplitude of current change cyclically. The two-dimensionality afforded by complex numbers provides a practical method for simultaneously enumerating both changes.

You do not need to master this aspect of mathematics to appreciate its applicability. As you read the next section of this chapter, use your hand-held telephone to play a digitally recorded song through your miniaturized ear buds. Personally experience this demonstration of an almost unbelievable truth of this real world. The musical sound that you hear is real even though the orchestra behind it is nowhere near. The square root of negative one helped make that happen! Simultaneous enumeration using both the real numbers and the imaginary numbers is practical and purposeful in this world.

Imaginary Numbers and Extra Dimensions of Space?

We sense three dimensions of space – always three dimensions and only three dimensions of space. Our three dimensions of space can be perceived as left/right, front/back, and up/down. For brevity, we can simply call these the X, Y and Z dimensions of space. Things can be arranged in any unique combination of three coordinate values describing their placement in space. No two material things can assume exactly the same coordinates for space at the same time. A collision - a direct physical interaction - occurs when two objects attempt to possess the same three coordinates of space at the same time.

During the 20th century, we came to understand that the space of our universe is expansive beyond the scope of imagination for almost all persons living in earlier ages. On a cosmic scale, the lengths of number lines for selection of values of X, Y and Z coordinates are without known limit. Our Milky Way galaxy is composed of about 100 billion stars spaced an average of five light years away from each other. As vast as the Milky Way is, this is just one of billions of similar galaxies. While we have measured a limit beyond which we have not yet received incoming light, we have not actually measured an outward boundary of space. Clearly, our realm of spacetime includes a lot of space.

So, where would a separate realm like heaven be placed? To ancient humanity, the idea of heaven separated from Earth required nothing more than the expectation of its location high above the clouds of our sky. The modern understanding of space renders absurd the idea of a heavenly realm separated from Earth simply as a function of distance. No matter how far we might travel away from this planet, we will not have traveled far enough to leave the grand, continuous universe defined by our three real-number dimensions of space. However, along with awareness that one cannot travel far enough to leave this universe, 20th century science also revealed signs that at least one additional dimension of space truly does exist somewhere, somehow. Placement of extra dimensions remains a mystery.

Since 1919, Einstein's field equations of relativity theory have predicted the presence of at least a 5th dimension of spacetime. In Einstein's field equations, the assumption of at least one additional dimension of space causes the forces of gravity and electromagnetism to mathematically merge in the same way that electricity and magnetism were mathematically merged in the late 19th century. The merger of forces works this way.

As it stands, the attractive forces of both gravity and electromagnetism decrease with increased distance of separation. Specifically they both fall off at the rate of the square of the distance of separation, or d^2. This is a function of distance raised to a power valued at 1 less than the number of dimensions of space. While the

d^2 condition satisfies Einstein's field equations for the fall of gravity and electromagnetism as a function of distance of separation squared, the d^2 condition does not cause gravity and electromagnetism to behave the same in the balance of several other field equations. However, if one additional dimension of space existed, then these equations would be calculated using a d^3 assumption. Under that assumption, gravity and electromagnetism both satisfy all the projections of Einstein's field equations. That is what is meant by the mathematical merger of gravity and electromagnetism. This is achieved under a d^3 assumption and that is a strong mathematical signal worthy of consideration. That signals the plausibility that the full cosmic structure includes at least one additional dimension of space beyond the three dimensions of space that we sense physically.

This mathematical finding was first published by Polish physicist Theodor Kaluza almost immediately after Einstein's second paper on relativity theory. Einstein initially rejected, and always resisted, Kaluza's ideas that relativity theory predicts at least one additional realm of spacetime. Today, however, many scientists give significant credence to the idea of at least one more dimension of spacetime.

In the decades since Einstein's death, the work of a new generation of thinkers has rekindled interest and research into additional dimensions of space and time.[41] It now seems certain that this cosmos includes at least one additional dimension of space. Today, a branch of theoretical physics called string theory predicts that even more than five dimensions of spacetime exist. Kaluza's original work involved the merger of gravity with electromagnetism with math

---

[41] Greene, Brian R. The Elegant Universe: Superstrings, Hidden Dimensions, and the Quest for the Ultimate Theory, W.W. Norton & Company, Inc., New York, 1999. ISBN 0-393-04688-5

assuming a fifth dimension of spacetime (1 dimension of time and 4 dimensions of space). With at least six total dimensions of space and time, the merger of forces becomes even more complete. With six or more dimensions of space and time, modern superstring mathematics completes the merger of all four distinct forces of nature (gravity, electromagnetism, strong nuclear force, and weak nuclear force). That mathematical merger appears strongest if one assumes the total number of dimensions of space is 10 (d^9). Some models suggest as many as 26 (d^{25}) total dimensions for space.

The math supporting at least one additional dimension of space is as sound as that supporting relativity theory, but lacks experimental confirmation. One practical obstacle is that no one can easily identify a place to hold all that extra space. Where, exactly, could one or more extra dimensions be held? This universe spans more than 13.7 billion light years in all directions from Earth. Simply moving further away cannot reasonably be expected to provide the answer to the physical placement of even a single extra dimension. Another answer is needed.

The most commonly voiced explanation for placement of additional dimensions dates back to an idea first proposed in the late 1920s. Swedish physicist, Oskar Klein, followed the original mathematical work of Theodor Kaluza and suggested that an additional dimension of space might be concealed within the very tiny scale of the Planck length. Originally taught by Max Planck in 1900, the Planck length is the smallest of all fractions of length. It is like the basic atom of space. Length cannot be cut into fractions smaller than the Planck length. Klein suggested that an additional dimension of space is wrapped up within a framework created by adjacent Planck lengths. This is popularly visualized as the wedging of tennis balls inside each open grid of a chain link fence. Imagine this as tennis balls within every space in a 2-dimensional stretch of a chain link fence. Complete the mental image by visualizing that fencing material stacked into a 3-dimensional pile. The tennis balls represent the extra dimension of space tucked into invisible recesses within our perceived dimensions of space. Placement of an extra dimension wrapped up circularly within that sub-Planck space is the concept now called Kaluza-Klein space, and flippantly nicknamed "inner space."

Kaluza-Klein space remains the leading candidate for the location of an extra dimension(s) of space but it really does not solve the problem. It does, however, allow modern physicists to speak of additional dimensions without taking the personal risk of proposing a specific alternative that could be ridiculed.

The rounded shape of a tennis ball in the chain-link model helps us visualize the idea of an extra dimension in some real location that is not exactly in our reach. However, Kaluza-Klein space really does not fully solve the original problem, and that original problem is getting even tougher to solve. Modern theories suggest there is more than one additional dimension of space. Under superstring theory, Kaluza-Klein space would be called upon to cram not one, but multiple dimensions of space into the framework of inner space. Instead of tennis balls, inner space might need to hold some type of advanced geometric shape with complex interfolding. Such shapes exist in the high mathematics and these shapes are called Calabi-Yau manifolds. Mathematically, all of this stuff seems compelling, but today there still is no practical idea for testing or confirming any of the many variations on the possible mathematical models for these ideas.

The problem is that Kaluza-Klein space introduces tougher problems than those which it proposes to solve. Even the simplest of models for placement of one or more additional dimensions of space within the sub-Planck grid stretches the limits of credibility because this breaks two fundamental principles of the physics for our world. The placement of additional dimensions within the sub-Planck grid of our spacetime ignores the fundamental expectation that the sub-Planck length cannot be further divided. Acceptance of an extra dimension of space, complete with incremental coordinates, requires that sub-Planck space can be subdivided within that space. This idea violates a fundamental precept of quantum theory and a fundamental precept of relativity. Within quantum theory, the idea that sub-Planck space can't be divided is not an experimental limit but a fundamental precept. Within relativity, a fundamental precept is that the laws of physics are the same from every frame of reference. If sub-Planck space is indivisible from our frame of reference, then it must be indivisible within the sub-Planck frame of reference. The truth is that inner space is simply not a good answer for the location of additional realms of spacetime.

Kaluza-Klein continues to receive consideration as a location for additional dimensions largely because no one has been willing to face the embarrassment of proposing a serious option. However, it is time to break that box. Confident in the word of God, those of faith can boldly consider models under which this universe is supplemented by a heavenly realm that will satisfy the biblical characterization of being "not of this world."

To consider the various options for solution of this problem it is useful to ask, "What does it mean to be here, there, or anywhere?" That answer sets the stage for the next question which is, "What does it mean

to be somewhere else?" Separate realms of existence will satisfy the meaning of being somewhere else, some place not of this world. The Lorentz-Fitzgerald equations will lead the way.

Let's return to our understanding of placement in space as the possession of a specific set of real-number coordinates for the X, Y, and Z dimensions of space at any given time. Two material objects can assume adjacent locations but cannot occupy the same place at the same time. This concept is so obvious that it hides in plain sight a potential mechanism for constructing more than one separate realm of spacetime. Knowing the immense scope of the dimensions of this universe, it is unreasonable to expect that a location outside this spacetime is a simply a place far, far away from "here." No matter how far away one travels, the values for the X, Y, Z, coordinates of space will just be another one of the limitless combinations of real numbers defining placement in this realm. And with that thought, the box can be broken.

> *Getting to a place outside our spacetime*
> *might not depend on how far one travels*
> *but on how fast one travels.*

Getting to a place outside our spacetime could be accomplished by assigning an imaginary number for any one of the coordinates for the X, Y, or Z dimensions of space or the dimension of time. Attaining superluminal velocity would make that happen.

For more than 100 years, science may have missed the full message taught by the Lorentz-Fitzgerald equations. When actual velocity becomes faster than the speed of light, the corrected values for mass, time and length shift from the set of real numbers to the set of imaginary numbers. Einstein taught that this signaled an absolute limit for travel speed. I think Einstein was wrong. I think the shift to imaginary numbers explains the location for the 5th or higher dimension(s). Any energy traveling faster than the speed of Einstein's light, and any mass precipitated from that superluminal energy, would have no place within our physical spacetime. Superluminal velocity would establish a set of coordinates that are someplace else. These coordinates would be 'not of this world.'

A realm using imaginary numbers for one or more coordinates of location would be separate from our realm but completely 'real.' One or more separate realms of existence could lie outside our spacetime even while sharing one or two real number coordinates with our spacetime. In this sense, separate realms would be like adjacent rooms and these rooms could be every bit as expansive as our real-number-times-four realm. The location for these separate rooms would be unperceived but would be real, truthfully described as literally 'in our midst.' All this requires is allowance for transmission of some type(s) of energy at any speed faster than Einstein's light.

The math of Kaluza suggested a rotational characteristic for the 5th dimension and this is exactly what one gets from the imaginary numbers. The imaginary numbers inherently demonstrate a pattern of circular spiraling as values progress through the steady increase of exponential powers (squared, cubed, etc.).

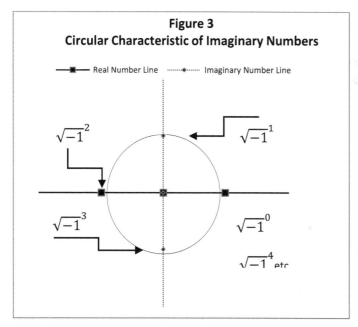

Figure 3
Circular Characteristic of Imaginary Numbers

$$\sqrt{-1}^0 = +1, \ \sqrt{-1}^1 = \sqrt{-1}, \ \sqrt{-1}^2 = -1, \ \sqrt{-1}^3 = -\sqrt{-1}, \ \sqrt{-1}^4 = +1 \ again, \text{ etc.}$$

As represented by Figure 3 above, the progression of the power series for imaginary numbers is circular, not curvilinear. Any number taken to the 1st power is itself, so $\sqrt{-1}^1 = \sqrt{-1}$ on the imaginary number line (the Y-axis running vertically). Squaring any square root is the same as leaving the original value unchanged, so $\sqrt{-1}^2$ returns us back to the real number line at the value of -1 (The X axis running horizontally). Continuing the power series to the 3rd power takes us back to the imaginary number line but on the negative side of zero ($-\sqrt{-1}$). The 4th power of the square root of negative 1 completes the cycle back to the real number line at the value of positive one. This is the same value as the square root of negative one raised to the zeroth power (for those who hated logarithms in school, know that you will not be tested on this by me). Continuation of this expansion through the 5th, 6th, 7th, and higher powers simply continues to wrap around this same counterclockwise cycle just as the 4th power returned to the same value as the zeroth power. The values for non-integer powers such as the 3.789th power represent points on the perfect circle that passes through all four of the index points shown graphically in Figure 3. What this means is that the imaginary numbers introduce a never-ending circular pattern upon exponential expansion, like the wrapped-up, cylindrical condition for the 5th dimension as expected by Kaluza and Klein. What this also shows is that the power series for the imaginary numbers can support enumeration of values that are either imaginary, or real. The power series for real numbers never yields a value outside the set of real numbers.

How Might Extra Dimensions Appear?

If at least one coordinate for space or time is enumerated using anything other than real numbers, then the close approximation between an object of this realm and one from an adjacent realm would appear like a rendezvous gone wrong. Objects of this realm and objects from other realms might come as close as sharing two dimensions of spacetime but the simultaneous sharing of all four coordinates of spacetime is impossible. Direct physical touching of an object from this realm with an object from an adjacent realm cannot occur because a complete sharing of all dimensions **valued in the set of real numbers** cannot occur.

Objects in adjacent realms of space would appear invisible, ghostly, and completely dark to our typical detectors. Detection of light through either biological or instrumental devices is based upon some form of physical interaction between the detector and the detected. Literally, the light from a detected object and some form of light detector must touch at the same exact set of X, Y, Z, and t coordinates for space and time within our realm. Superluminal energy and matter will not intersect with all four real-number values for the X, Y, Z, and t coordinates used for our real-world detectors. Therefore, superluminal energy and matter would be completely dark to typical real-world detectors.

Dark matter and dark energy cannot be seen by our typical analytical instruments but are indirectly measurable through gravitational effects. This suggests that dark energy and dark matter do not demonstrate coordinates for space and time using the same set of numbers that defined our realm. The simplest explanation for this behavior is that dark energy and dark matter represent something superluminal.

(Note: Since we can detect dark energy and dark matter through gravitational but not light-based signals, the practicing physicist might consider this as a sign that gravity acts at superluminal velocity.)

Those who believe in heaven expect a realm that is real, not visible from our current frame of reference, and capable of supporting literal resurrection and life in a physical body, a remade, immortal body. A material realm that truly exists but cannot be seen is exactly what one would expect for a world made from light that travels faster than Einstein's light. Both immaterial and material characteristics could be expected of this realm, just as we experience immaterial energy and resting matter in our current, mortal realm of existence.

Assumption that the Lorentz-Fitzgerald equations remain as valid above the speed of Einstein's light as below that speed has been blocked for too long by blind loyalty to Einstein's worldview. Today, there is no reason to assume that physics breaks down above the speed of light. If we consider what happens above the speed of

Einstein's light, we would expect that superluminal energy could take on the characteristics of matter as a function of its speed relative to the speed of Einstein's light (the c of e=mc²). Above the speed of light we should expect that corrected values for mass, length, and time would demonstrate a mirror image of that seen in our spacetime. Figure 4 shows the calculation for the Lorentz-Fitzgerald correction for mass both above and below the speed of Einstein's light. (For practical purposes, the imaginary values above the speed of light are reflected graphically as the real number equivalent.)

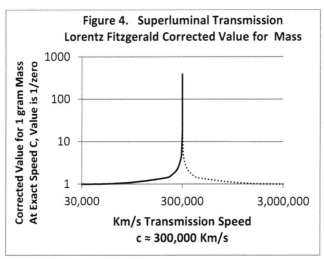

Figure 4. Superluminal Transmission Lorentz Fitzgerald Corrected Value for Mass

Figure 4 demonstrates the results of calculation of the Lorentz-Fitzgerald equations both above and below the speed of light. (The imaginary values above 300,000 Km/s are displayed as the real number absolute value. The true imaginary system value is restored by multiplication of the graphed number by the square root of negative one). Below the exact speed of Einstein's light, the numeric range of the Lorentz-Fitzgerald results involves entirely real numbers. Above the exact speed of Einstein's light, the numeric range of these equations involve only the imaginary numbers. Exactly at the speed of Einstein's light, there is a mathematical abyss, the undefined state of division by zero. (This interruption caused by division by zero cannot be seen graphically on a scale that also reflects the important j-hook curves of these functions.)

The upward j-hook that takes shape around 90% to 99% below the speed of Einstein's light would be expected to reverse at transmission speeds about 101% to 110% of the speed of Einstein's light. Within plus or minus 10% of the speed of Einstein's light, the slope of the function is nearly vertical and the expected characteristics of matter in this range would be similar to those of subatomic particles. More than 10% above or below c, the slope of this physical relationship is very horizontal. At an energy transmission velocity faster than 110% that of Einstein's light, material structure would be as solid as anything in our realm.

(Superluminal massive objects like planets could collectively travel slower than the speed of light (c) but still demonstrate superluminal characteristics if the subatomic particles that form them retain the essential energy equivalence of the superluminal pure energy from which they were formed.)

Acceptance of the Lorentz-Fitzgerald equations at all values, including those above the speed of Einstein's light is all that is needed to explain a mechanism that could define at least one additional realm of existence. Light that travels as slowly as Einstein's light would form one realm – this realm – and light that travels faster would form one or more separate realms. Separation of those realms would be based upon the ability or inability to cross the chasm created by the division by zero.

This model is based upon nothing other than the expectation that the Lorentz-Fitzgerald equation does not suddenly fail when faced with light of a higher power than Einstein's light. This model is strikingly congruent with an image recorded about 2000 years ago as a parable presented by Christ.

There was a rich man who dressed in purple garments and fine linen and dined sumptuously each day. And lying at his door was a poor man named Lazarus, covered with sores, who would gladly have eaten his fill of the scraps that fell from the rich man's table. Dogs even used to come and lick his sores. When the poor man died, he was carried away by angels to the bosom of Abraham. The rich man also died and was buried, and from the netherworld, where he was in torment, he raised his eyes and saw Abraham far off and Lazarus at his side. And he cried out, 'Father Abraham, have pity on me. Send Lazarus to dip the tip of his finger in water and cool my tongue, for I am suffering torment in these flames.' Abraham replied, 'My child, remember that you received what was good during your lifetime while Lazarus likewise received what was bad; but now he is comforted here, whereas you are tormented. **Moreover, between us and you a great chasm is established to prevent anyone from crossing who might wish to go from our side to yours or from your side to ours.'** Luke 16:19-26

This parable shares a lot of important information, including the expectation for afterlife involving more than one separated realms of existence. A realm of paradise is held separate from an unpleasant realm of isolation. Between the two realms is a chasm not passable even by one as important as Abraham. Could it be that this parable reveals knowledge of that which can be envisioned only through an understanding of the scientific findings of the 20th century? If this universe really does hold an additional realm separated on the basis of speed of energy transmission, then there would indeed be a chasm of separation between them. That chasm would be the physical result of division by zero at the exact speed of Einstein's light.

How Might One Test the Reality of Superluminal Realms?

If realms are differentiated based on the speed of signal transmission, then the lack of shared coordinates will represent both the finding to be measured and the complication preventing measurement. A superluminal object would have at least one coordinate enumerated using an imaginary number. As such, that superluminal object would never physically interact with any typical detector at any place in our system of real-number coordinates for X, Y, Z and time.

One could employ highly sensitive detectors shielded valiantly from interfering signals and still expect to find no significant interaction even if bombarded by massive streams of superluminal particles. However, it is possible that rare energy fluctuations across the threshold separating Einstein's light from superluminal light could occur. If superluminal matter exists, then isolated particles might rarely demonstrate a random slowing to subluminal speed. With highly sensitive detectors exquisitely protected from outside interference, these rare events might be detectable. Indeed, a modern detector has been developed that very rarely detects a type of mass flippantly named WIMPs (weakly interacting massive particles). The detailed characteristics of this type of particle have not yet been explained but this could represent a sign of the boundary state between this and a superluminal realm.

I can envision a different way to look for signs of an interface between this realm and a superluminal realm. Attempting to measure the very rare slowing of a boundary particle from the superluminal side to the subluminal realm forces the analyst to detect and interpret rare events that are not experimentally controlled. It would appear more likely that one could interpret potential jumps across the light-speed barrier if those jumps were initiated from within our realm under full experimental control. Indeed, it is possible that this experiment has already been conducted hundreds of times without realizing it. It is reasonable to expect that high-energy collisions of subatomic particles could demonstrate a slight but measurable loss of mass resulting from the collision. This would be the result of the acceleration of minor fractions of the collided particles to superluminal velocity. Having been accelerated beyond a superluminal velocity, that minor fraction of total mass should show up as a loss of total system energy measured by detectors within our realm. This would happen only in trace fractions of the total mass and might be interpreted simply as a random measurement error in individual experiments. However, we would expect that the fluctuation is not random. We would expect that loss of energy is significantly more common than energy gain. Furthermore, when collision conditions are systematically modified to span a range from lower to higher collision energy, the measured loss would be expected to change systematically from lower to higher values. Detection of a pattern of systematic increase in energy loss with higher energy impact would be consistent with the conclusion that a quark or three were literally knocked out of the park!

It is important to clarify that I do not believe that more than trace amounts of subluminal matter would ever become accelerated to superluminal speed. I fully accept that the matter formed from Einstein's light cannot be accelerated beyond the speed constraints of Einstein's light. However, every physical boundary has a little variability surrounding it. In the experiment presented above, I propose that a very small fraction, simply a trace, of the energy liberated by very high-speed subatomic collisions would become lost to this world by acceleration to velocity in slight excess of c.

What Does This Mean to This Man of Faith?

What this means is that even at its frontier, science is more supportive of faith than of atheism. We have previously reviewed the data that confirm that this universe was created. Now we have reviewed a topic at the cutting edge of science that supports the plausibility of an additional realm of spacetime, a realm consistent with heaven.

The exact mechanism that I have proposed here might fail scientific confirmation in all details, but it is reasonable to expect that we will find a viable mechanism for establishing at least one separate realm of spacetime. We can expect this to be true because the math of Einstein's relativity theory says it is true. Einstein's relativity theory points mathematically to an expanding universe, time dilation, gravitational lensing, and at least one additional dimension of spacetime. With 3/4 of these relativistic predictions already confirmed, we can be confident that there really is at least one additional dimension of spacetime.

I have proposed that superluminal energy could represent a simple mechanism for enumeration of coordinates for a separate realm of spacetime supportive of dark matter and dark energy. **This does not**

mean that the reality of God turns on the question of whether there is or is not superluminal energy transmission. This is one possible mechanism. It might be completely correct, completely wrong, or something in between. Regardless of the detailed mechanism, it is reasonable to expect that we will find at least one additional realm of existence beyond this spacetime. In that way, both modern science and ancient faith point in the same direction.

As we approach the end of this book, I ask the reader, especially the skeptical reader, to reflect on the evidence as it stands. Many intelligent people who are not trained scientists believe that expert scientists have functionally disproven God. If you are of this mindset, let me ask you to address these questions. **What scientific fact disproves God? What fact has been omitted from this book that would have otherwise disproven the existence of God?** If you are truthful, you must acknowledge that there is no fact that disproves the existence of God.

Atheists can present arguments against organized religion but failures of organized religion do not constitute evidence against God. Atheists can present hypotheses for explaining the natural phenomena without crediting God but this does not represent evidence against God. The truth is that accumulated data from a wide variety of modern measurements consistently render purely atheistic explanations less credible with each passing decade. The scientific probability of the formation of this universe exactly as it is in the absence of God is now so low as to deserve statistical rejection under any unbiased analysis plan. The truth is that modern science does not argue against the possibility of God. Modern science provides reinforcement for faith, including faith in additional cosmic realms like heaven.

Chapter 8. Atheism is a Great Big Lie

Except for the discussion of untested mechanisms for coordinates of separate realms of spacetime, this book has addressed facts of science that are confirmed and well accepted. We have reviewed the mathematical foundation of the Lorentz-Fitzgerald equations confirmed by the operation of our GPS navigation systems. These equations showed us that theological concepts such as timelessness (time undefined) and omnipresence (distance unit = zero) truly apply to pure energy transmitted at the speed of Einstein's light. We then used the Lorentz-Fitzgerald equations to derive Einstein's famous equation, $e=mc^2$. This allowed us to personally understand how matter could have been created from no prior matter. We reviewed the sequence of steps through which this world actually came to be and recognized that the measurements of science perfectly match the ancient scriptures of Genesis Chapter 1. Through this work, we support a data-driven conclusion that science does not conflict with faith, but actually supports it. Modern humanity has been granted a clearer physical demonstration of God's reality than that enjoyed by most prior generations.

All that said, resistance to faith is widespread. Atheism is popular. If I have shared the truth, why is faith actively, broadly, and vehemently opposed by scientific leaders with credentials well above mine? Part of this answer deals with mistakes of organized religion and we will address that. However, most of this answer deals with the fact that atheism is based upon a great big lie, the most ancient of all lies.

Atheism is not to be confused with nagging personal doubt. Active atheism is full out, unrestrained opposition to God. What could possibly motivate such opposition? The answer lies in the fact that faith is not simply a question of whether a person chooses to believe in God, but whether a person accepts subservience to God. Understand that, and you understand the motivation and tactics of the active atheist. The more impressed one is with one's self, the more difficult it is to accept the role of the employee, the servant, the ruled rather than the ruler. Great intellect brings risk of personal arrogance, of foolishness in the biblical sense. Biblical foolishness is on display today within the ranks of those who fancy themselves as smarter than others.

A full understanding of the reality of God brings one face to face with an understanding of the reality of Satan, God's most powerful adversary. Satan has refused subservience to God and has set in motion the serious disruption of cosmic peace. You and I have been swept up in this disruption of peace. Having suffered defeat and expulsion from the realm of heaven, Satan has only one remaining tactic with which to lash out in revenge against God. Inflicting harmful disruption into the relationship between God and humanity is Satan's last act of antagonism toward the King he rejects. Misdirection of humanity is Satan's mechanism of attack, and humanity is routinely willing to go along. The greatest lie of all time involves Satan's attempts to get humanity to think and act as though we are the boss, the independent judge of all that should be called 'good' and that which should be called 'wrong.' That was the crux of the first lie from Satan to humanity and that general theme continues to play well to this day.

Satan can't strike back at God directly, but can broadcast ideas that misdirect humans, driving a wedge between us and our Creator. The misuse of science to direct people away from God is one of the great examples of misdirection today. That said, the misuse of religion is even more timeless and has collectively caused even greater harm. Misuse of religion fuels active human resistance against God.

I will not direct a lot of space to the detailed itemization of examples of the misuse of religion and the misbehavior of the religious. The failures of religion and of the religious have been thoroughly covered in the books of some of the most active atheists. The reader is referred to the many works of Christopher Hitchens[42], Richard Dawkins[43], David Silverman[44], Sam Harris[45], or Victor Stenger[46]. In their arguments against God, these atheists present a litany of past and recent misdeeds as though the failings of religious humans provide evidence against the reality of God. I could itemize the many examples of exaggeration by these authors. I could refute the instances of false association of blame across all creeds for examples of wrongdoing associated with a single creed. I could demonstrate how examples of the past are made to sound worse through extrapolation of 21st century social standards onto primitive or medieval periods of social development. (The application of modern social standards to past ages of social structure is unreasonable under either theistic or atheistic worldviews.) However, itemization of exaggeration and errors of logic demonstrated by these atheists would not optimize the pursuit of truth. The truth is that every possible sin has been committed by those who claim to act in the service of God. Religions and the religious are guilty of some of the worst acts of humans against other humans. These sins are not simply the product of past mistakes. The pedophilic scandals of the Catholic Church do not represent past behavior alone, but represent widespread sin today. The news over the last several decades carries sufficient examples to demonstrate that sin from within organized religion is not limited to Roman Catholicism.

In some cases, the harm caused by religion is not a classic sin, but theological error that leads to a loss in credibility for faith. Such has been the case with the self-inflicted battles between faith and science during the 20th century. The strident insistence on a creation

---

[42] Previously referenced: Christopher Hitchens, God is Not Great.

[43] Previously referenced: Richard Dawkins, The God Delusion.

[44] Previously referenced: David Silverman, Fighting God

[45] Previously referenced: Sam Harris, Letter to a Christian Nation and The End of Faith

[46] Previously referenced: Victor Stenger, God, The Failed Hypothesis.

sequence lasting only six days and timed only 10,000 years ago causes the same harm as the Roman Catholic prosecution of Galileo. Strident insistence that the big bang did not happen demonstrates willful ignorance in face of overwhelming evidence. This might seem to reflect steadfast faith in the face of adversity, but I have to wonder at times whether there isn't also a significant component of self-serving arrogance. It is one thing to admit that the Galileo affair was wrong, but that can easily be attributed to 'those bad old Catholics.' Young-earth creationism is primarily a protestant issue, largely an American protestant issue, so reversal on that point can't just be shirked as an error of 'the other guy.' Review of current justifications for young-earth theology demonstrates a motivation of self-preservation, exactly like that of the medieval church in the time of Galileo. In a paraphrase, 'if people stop believing in creation exactly as we have taught, they will start questioning everything else we have taught.'

That is not justifiable. It is wrong. God has not designed this world with false signs of age. Truth does not conflict with truth. God does not deceive His creatures. The truth is that God did create this world, exactly as portrayed in the Bible, but not as an instantaneous act of divine fiat. God created this world by bringing forth light and shaping that light according to the natural mechanisms that we measure today. God did this, but He did not do this on a time frame of six consecutive earthdays. When religions teach details regarding the interpretation of the Genesis scriptures that are clearly wrong, they misdirect people away from faith. The errors of modern religions misdirect people away from faith just as certainly as does any action of the atheists.

The absolute error of insistence on a creation sequence only six current earth-days in duration is the single greatest reason for the widespread view that the scriptures cannot be believed. Indeed, the only reason this book has been pursued to completion is that I do not find others defending the fact that the opening chapter of scriptures is truly credible! When challenged by an atheist like Victor Stenger for evidence of the reality of God, it should be a simple matter to point to the Genesis scriptures and take full credit for the fact that these scriptures reflect 'dangerous prophecy' that has been confirmed. We can trust that these are not the words of pre-scientific humans and we know that the match between these scriptures and modern science is not the work of humans intent on self-fulfillment. **We can trust that these words reflect knowledge beyond humanity. This should mean something to all of us.**

Those of faith are spending our entire effort as though we still live in the 19th century. We act as though the Genesis scriptures describe a creation event that did not actually happen as described. We act as though we believe in God despite inadequacy of the scriptures. We do this because of arrogance. We do this because of the incorrect but tenacious interpretation of the meaning of one ambiguous word. Books directed toward the defense of the faith argue for the reality of God on the basis of indirect evidence. Books retreat from the defense of the Genesis scriptures as though there is no match between these ancient teachings and the facts of modern science. That is absolutely needless! The truth is that the science of the 20th and 21st centuries allows us to point directly to Genesis Chapter 1 as the primary source of evidence for God, when we correctly interpret those scriptures. The Hebrew word, 'Yom,' can mean any period of time and is fully consistent with the day-age interpretation of the Genesis scriptures. **The truth is that Genesis Chapter 1 reads as the literal truth when you don't take the wrong word literally.**

Atheists wield the errors of the faithful as weapons against faith. We need to stop giving God's adversaries reason to justifiably criticize His loyalists. That said, it is important to realize that failures of the religious and the institutions they support do not represent evidence against the existence of God. The attacks of the atheists against religions should give a reason for self-review among the religious; however, these are false attacks against the reality of God. The arguments of the atheists are scientifically falsifiable and they have been falsified. Continuation of the argument that science and reason argue against faith in God represents a lie. **Those who believe that argument have been misled and those who teach it mislead.**

I can't pick a more easily dissected example of the misleading summary of popularized science than the work of the self-professed atheist, Lawrence Krauss. In his book, <u>A Universe From Nothing: Why There is Something From Nothing</u>[47] Krauss demonstrates multiple obvious examples of untrue atheistic arguments. The types of untrue arguments displayed by Krauss include:

1. Illogical personal endorsement. 'If You Want to Be Smart Like Me, Don't Believe In God'
2. Falsification of Truth While Claiming to Be Truthful
3. Argument that Objective Measurement is the Only Source of Real Truth
4. Supporting One Hypothesis with Data that Actually Support the Other

In this book, Krauss presents a popularized summary of cosmology and physics that shows that all matter in this universe came from nothing. He summarizes mathematical interpretations of the WMAP confirmation of dark matter. He truthfully teaches that the visible matter of our universe is a minor fraction of the total mass of the cosmos. He blends in other facts or possibilities that are not within easy reach of most and then extrapolates to a larger scale, creating a false impression of an argument against the possibility of God. One example is the teaching of observations of the details of the hydrogen atom, the smallest and simplest of all atomic elements. The electron cloud of the hydrogen atom appears to demonstrate fleeting quantum fluctuations in which an extra electron along with its anti-electron burst into separate existence for a microsecond, quickly recombining with no net change in matter content (returning to

---

[47] Krauss, Lawrence M. *A Universe from Nothing: Why There Is Something Rather Than Nothing* (2012), Atria Books, ISBN 978-1-4516-2445-8

a zero-sum condition). He then summarizes an extrapolation of a quantum fluctuation on the larger scale of the whole cosmos. He demonstrates that it is possible that all the matter of this universe popped into existence from nothing on a huge scale. A universe popping into existence would have been initiated in the form of light (a photon can be split into two parts, a particle and its antiparticle. When a particle and antiparticle recombine, the result is a restored photon, the quantum unit of light). He summarizes the possibility that almost all particles and anti-particles formed from an initial burst of light would recombine back into pure light. He theorizes that a slight excess of particles relative to anti-particles became established (with no justification, since the zero sum game requires an exact 1-to-1 match between particles versus antiparticles). He proceeds to theorize that the excess particles that did not recombine with anti-particles might be the raw material that formed all matter held in this cosmos today. He notes that an alternative option might have been that particles and anti-particles formed in the expected 1-to-1 ratio with recombination prevented due to an unexplained separation of particles from antiparticles into separate realms of existence. In that alternative mechanism, one realm (our world) might be formed by particles while another realm would be made from antiparticles. (This matches the idea of separation of light into two distinct pools which I discussed in a previous chapter). Krauss posits that, through one of these two mechanisms, the rearrangement of a pool of no raw materials, using the net expenditure of zero energy, yielded today's huge collection of something derived from nothing. Without factual resolution of the issue, he then concludes and editorializes that his understanding of this mechanism eliminates the need for God as an explanation for creation.

Think about that. Science (or the possibilities within science) has been summarized as a set of individual plausible truths only to be closed by a blatantly false conclusion! If a person does not follow the details closely, it could certainly seem as though he/she had read a strong argument against God. That would not be the truth.

Krauss's explanation for something emerging from nothing is completely supportive of faith in *creatio ex nihilo*, creation from nothing! However, Dr. Krauss does not teach his audience this but chooses to teach the opposite. My academic credentials are well below the level of academic distinction earned by Dr. Krauss but I am sufficiently well trained to recognize a false argument when I see it. This is a false argument. To present this information with a conclusion that the facts argue against the reality of God is a blatant example of misleading science. Human understanding of the mechanisms of action within this universe is not evidence of the absence of God.

If You Want to Be Smart Like Me, You Won't Believe In God

Analyzed to its core, this work of Dr. Krauss is an easily dissected example of common propaganda tactics of atheism. The basic facts of science presented by Dr. Krauss are not false. However, a lie is told through the presentation of an editorial conclusion as though the absence of God was the only possibility supported by those facts. Every fact presented by Dr. Krauss supports the conclusion that creation from nothing is scientifically plausible. That is fully consistent with faith in our Creator and Krauss falsely editorializes against that conclusion. It is important to recognize the false nature this type of propaganda technique that can be paraphrased like this:

> 'Look at me. I am very smart. I am as smart as anyone can be. I am smarter than you. I bet you don't even understand all that I have laid out for you in this book. I know all this and I do not believe in God. If you want to be smart like me, you will not believe in God.'

Do not be fooled. Sounding smart is not the same as drawing valid conclusions. Krauss has not drawn a valid conclusion from these facts. His facts do not argue against God. The facts that he summarizes actually support faith.

Falsification of Truth While Claiming to Be Truthful

Truth is the shared pursuit of the scientist and the faithful. Truthful measurement, truthful analysis, and truthful reporting are the duties of every scientist. That duty is often shirked.

Unjustified ridicule and derision with unsupported falsehoods are commonly levied against the faithful by active atheists. Dr. Krauss employs this tactic throughout his book. Let me point out one such instance. At one point, Dr. Krauss charged that faith in God is supported by no evidence. At one point, he described God as 'hocus pocus.' Balance these assertions against the fact that Dr. Krauss had just explained the scientific evidence confirming the centuries-old belief in *creatio ex nihilo.* What scientific or logical principle was used to justify Krauss's assertion that God is a 'hocus pocus' being for whom there is no evidence? The answer is, none.

Krauss might have asserted that he does not accept this evidence as *adequate proof* of God. However, he cannot truthfully teach that there is no evidence of God. The truth is that the existence of God is supported by substantial evidence and Krauss's own work constitutes some of that evidence. To falsely teach that there is no evidence for God is an abuse of the trust given to those of high academic rank. Most people simply will not drill down on the details presented by credentialed experts. However, when you do, you find that Dr. Krauss (as with others) is misleading.

Argument that Objective Measurement is the Only Real Truth

Dr. Krauss takes the opportunity to editorialize his view that objective measurement is the only valid way of knowing truth. He claims that objective measurement is superior to revelation and intergenerational tradition. However, Dr. Krauss's discussion of the far-reaching implications of an expanding universe illustrates the failure of objective measurement as the only source of truth.

Through measurements that were infeasible before the 20th century, we can be absolutely certain that this universe had a beginning. The expansion of the universe represents one of the measurable facts that prove this. However, the distant galaxies that currently demonstrate this universe to be expanding will, in the future, expand away from Earth so fast that their light will never again reach us. Then, we could never again measure the truth of an expanding universe. Today's truth will not simply become invisible; it will become falsified. In the future, this expanding universe will falsely appear to be static, even though it is expanding. Through Dr. Krauss's own example, we know that objective measurement using mechanical instruments made of the substances of this realm simply cannot reveal all that is true of the full cosmos. The truth is that this universe is expanding. When time has progressed to the point that today is ancient history, this truth can only be known through trans-generational teaching! This confirmed truth will be become the substance of ancient tradition!

God-of-the- Gaps; Another Example of Falsification of Truth

As with other atheists, Dr. Krauss parrots a charge that God is a man-made invention. He challenges that a "god-of-the-gaps" has been made up to satisfy a need to explain that which humanity does not understand. Krauss argues that reliance upon God is unnecessary because modern science allows us to understand the physical mechanisms through which our world works. Some might view this as a strong argument, but that is the illusion produced by blending elements of truth with a core message that is false. The fallacy of any half-true argument is that the false part cannot be made true simply by associating it with a true part. The truthful elements of the 'god-of-the-gaps' argument is that humans of essentially all cultures resort to religion, even if that is in pursuit of false gods. The untrue element is that this means that God, the God of the Bible, is a simple invention of humanity.

'God-of-the-gaps' is an absurd assertion that is backed by no factual data. To the contrary, the faithful believe in God because we have valid reason(s) to understand God as a true, immaterial, but communicative life-form. We have good reason to understand that God reveals His presence through verified scripture and through personal prayer.

While progressing from mankind's animalistic beginnings to our current modern condition, many cultures and subcultures have taught legends and actively worshiped false gods other than the God who spoke directly to Adam, Abraham and Moses. While atheists charge that a proliferation of pagan gods reflects a basic biological need to invent God, an alternative hypothesis is that this is exactly what we would expect if the God of the Bible is true while human fidelity to God's leadership is flawed.

What evidence can the atheist demonstrate to claim that humans have a biological need to invent God? The answer is that there is none. The atheist can point to nothing beyond circular logic to support the assertion that humanity needs to invent God. They point to the fact that humans of all cultures reach out to religion. However, they cannot point to evidence of a biological need for religion by non-human animals. (Expect that within 10 years after publication of this book, some atheist will counter that they have found signs of rudimentary religion among animals. Expect this evidence to be weak.) The truth is that demonstration of religious pursuit across all human cultures actually reflects the scriptural teaching that every human soul is known to God before the start of life within the womb. This means that every human soul also knows God, even if the crippling effects of life in this physical realm dulls that knowledge.

In contrast to the atheist's argument, the faithful have direct evidence that the God of Genesis Chapter 1 is real. We have reason to understand that God is both real and communicative. The reality of a communicative God explains why humans of all types gravitate toward God. No fact of science argues against that belief. Indeed the documented history of the Jews, the unique subset of humans who demonstrated the greatest fidelity toward trans-generational teaching, has revealed for all mankind the reality of God, our Creator. Through the faithful trans-generational teaching of the Jews, truthful knowledge of our Creator has been revealed to the benefit of any who will listen.

Long before humanity would know anything about germ theory, the Hebrews had been taught the importance of washing before eating. Long before we knew about the vectors of parasitic disease, the ancient Hebrews were taught that swine were not the safest of foods. Long before humanity knew this fact from the study of human DNA, the ancient Hebrews knew that mankind had once approached the edge of extinction. I don't know whether humanity survived that event of near-extinction through the use of a boat carrying every example of modern animal, but I know that the ancient Hebrews were aware of the reality of an event of near extinction for all but a small group of humans. The ancient Hebrews were aware of facts that modern man can now understand but the Hebrews knew these important lessons before science taught us those lessons. The ancient Hebrews knew these facts because, more so than any other group of humans, the ancient humans who would become the Hebrews listened to the messengers of God. They listened and they valued and they taught, passing God's word faithfully from generation to generation even in the face of adversity. Krauss can choose to not believe, but he cannot refute the assertion that humanity knows of God because God is both real and communicative.

Supporting One Hypothesis with Data that Support the Other

The most critical flaw in Dr. Krauss's work is the summarization of science that does not actually distinguish between either of two opposite hypotheses, then editorializing as though the facts support only one. Dr. Krauss violates the basic rules of the scientific method in this way but is comfortable in his expectation that most people will simply not drill down on his details. Non-scientists most often conclude that the smart scientist must be correct and trust that a highly credentialed scientist would never deceive. However, when you do drill down on the detail, you will find deception. Dr. Krauss has structured arguments that are completely misleading, completely indefensible. They meet the definition of deception.

The best I might grant is that the evidence presented in the book, <u>A Universe from Nothing</u>, might be argued to represent a tie, evidence supporting either of two opposing hypotheses: 'God is not real' or 'God is real.' However, Krauss does not argue this as a tie, but declares that our understanding of these facts argues against God. This is false. In truth, this work does not even represent a scientific tie. This work actually represents a clear win for the argument that **God Is Real!**

This is how the scientific method applies in this case. The only data-driven argument ever directed against faith was based upon that old misunderstanding of the law of conservation of matter. The argument was that our Creator could not be real because a creation event could not be real because matter could neither be created nor destroyed. The faithful believe that our Creator is real and did indeed create all that we see from nothing. We can apply the scientific method to reflect a contrast between these two mutually exclusive distinct hypotheses.

Null: The atheistic hypothesis states **"God is Not"**

Alternative: The theistic alternative states **"God Is."**

The evidence presented by Dr. Krauss shows that matter really can be created and that this entire universe really did emerge from a pool of no pre-existing matter. This evidence drives the scientific rejection of the null hypothesis, the atheistic hypothesis. The alternative hypothesis, the theistic hypothesis, remains unchallenged. The truth is that the work of Dr. Krauss factually refutes the atheistic world view and supports the scientific conclusion that **God Is!**

This is not the first loss for the atheistic hypothesis that 'God is Not.' The history of the 20th and 21st centuries has yielded nothing but a consistent series of losses for the foundations of atheism, and a string of wins for the conclusion that '**God Is!**'

The Driver of the Great Big Lie

It is now inarguable that this world really was created as something from nothing, with light as the first step, with the formation of the Sun-Earth-Moon system at the 4th step, with plant life before animal life, with sea life before terrestrial life, and with human life as the last major form of life to appear. It is undeniable that "**Energy is, therefore God could be.**" The full set of truths allow that possibility to be upgraded. The idea that God is possible can be upgraded to a conclusion that **God is scientifically plausible**. Any claim to the contrary, even when voiced by a well-credentialed scientist, is a great big lie.

Reality includes the recognition that, **if God is real, then Satan is too**. Since the beginning of the human experience, Satan has wreaked havoc upon humanity using the only tool available, misdirection. Whether bumped just slightly off course or twisted to complete opposition to God, interference between humanity and our Creator is the goal of that misdirection. This is the driver of that great big lie.

Don't Be Misled and Don't Mislead

Readers, please do not be misled and do not mislead others. Closely examine the facts of science within your reach. Use this book as a starting point but also read as many other authors as you can. Study the writings of atheists (referenced in the opening of this chapter) as well as those of faith. Try to find actual fact(s) that truly argue against the possibility of God. They are not there. When you drill down on the message of an atheistic scientist, you will find that their arguments against God are not supported by evidence of the absence of God. Personal rejection of God, a personal choice for atheism, is not evidence against God. Even for leading scientists, personal rejection of allegiance to God is not evidence against the reality of God.

The atheist can say that s/he does not personally believe in God and I can accept that as a demonstration of free will. What the atheist cannot do is claim that s/he does not believe in God because science says that God cannot be real. Science does not lead us away from God. Modern science leads us directly to God, our Creator, as introduced to humanity through the opening chapter of the Bible.

.

Chapter 9. Science Can Reinforce Our Faith

Truth does not conflict with truth. Our natural world is truly the work of God, so truthful observation of natural mechanisms will always reveal God's presence and His brilliance. Antagonism between science and faith is a self-inflicted malady. It is completely needless.

As a young college student, I was told by skeptics that the study of advanced physical and biological sciences would dash the foundations of my Roman Catholic upbringing. I found the opposite. As I learned more, I consistently found palpable reassurance of God's reality through examples of intelligence within the works of nature. The truth is that God's creative ingenuity and wisdom are on display whether the detailed field of study is chemistry, biology, or even something as intangible as math.

The truth is that those of us living today enjoy an opportunity not available in the past. In ways that have never been experienced before, God's world can be studied on a level of detail that can reveal His true presence. The match between modern knowledge and the creative sequence of Genesis Chapter 1 illustrated through the chapters of this book represents just the start. There is more to be enjoyed by those who embrace science from a foundation of faith.

Even those who do not choose science as a vocation will be well served to study popular science. Keep in mind that the atheists will pepper their books with chides and insults, but the facts presented will help you see God's world as it is. There are a number of authors, however, who write from a foundation of faith and I recommend these. Two authors that I highly recommend have been referenced previously in this text. Hugh Ross [48,49] and Gerald Schroeder, [50] should

---

[48] Ross, Hugh. The Creator and the Cosmos: How the Greatest Scientific Discovery of the Century Reveals the Existence of God. Colorado Springs, CO. NavPress Group, 1994. Print 3rd. ISBN 0891097007

be included in everyone's 'must-read' list. I rank these authors as two of the most important teachers for our day. Another interesting author is Michael Guillen[51]. Guillen extends the discussion of the interface between science and faith to many topics not included by others. You will enjoy his books and you will also enjoy the many instances of internet visibility for this author. A specific search to be recommended is the microscopic demonstration of the biochemical change immediately upon fertilization of a human egg. Paul Davies is another excellent teacher of popular science. Paul Davies is ostensibly an agnostic author, and he is an effective teacher who should be read[52]. Davies typically presents himself as an atheist, but he does try to present a balance for both sides of this topic. He does a fair job of providing a basis for understanding how the facts of science relate to the possibility of faith, just before closing each topic with a lame argument against faith. His arguments against faith are so lame that I sometimes have to wonder whether they were actually meant to support an understanding that atheism is not as reasonable as some would portray it. Brian Greene is another highly recommended teacher. Dr. Greene does not betray overt sympathy for either theist or atheist sentiments. Instead, he simply teaches from a foundation of a very deep understanding of the scientific mechanisms underlying this universe. [53]

Dr. Greene's work is not always easy to read, but after struggling through it, I came to appreciate a number of features of this universe that are just not described as well by any other author. Greene was the first author who allowed me to truly understand one of the

---

[49] Ross, Hugh. More than a Theory; Revealing a Testable Model for Creation. Grand Rapids, MI. Baker Books 2009

[50] Previously referenced: Gerald Schroeder The Science of God (and other works)

[51] Guillen, Michael. Amazing Truths: How Science and the Bible Agree. Zondervan, 2016 ISBN 9780310343769

[52] Previously referenced: Davies, Paul. The Mind of God (and other works)

[53] Greene Brian R. The Elegant Universe: Superstrings, Hidden Dimensions, and the Quest for the Ultimate Theory, W.W. Norton & Company, Inc., New York, 1999. ISBN 0-393-04688-5

deepest meanings of e=mc^2. In our realm of spacetime, everything travels at the speed of light. That sounds odd but it also is the foundation for a very good understanding of 'spacetime.' Spacetime is a merger of two words that means a lot more than simply the close association of space and time dimensions. Spacetime really does reflect an intimate, functional blend of 4 different dimensions into one common structure. This might be visualized as any 4 associated columns in a spreadsheet. The columns are distinct but not existent without the others. Three of the dimensions of our spacetime seem to be more alike than the 4th, but all 4 dimensions of spacetime are merged; they are functionally inseparable and somewhat interchangeable. Let's tackle this nuance and see how a deeper understanding of this detail can also lead to deeper reflection on our relationship with God.

Matter travels through space at a speed much lower than c of e=mc^2. Light travels through space at the full speed of c. Now, while traveling at the fastest possible speed through the dimensions of space, light does not travel at all through the dimension of time. For light in a vacuum, time is mathematically undefined. Light spends none of its energy equivalence traveling through the dimension of time, which is why it can travel both quickly and **invariably**, through space. (The invariable speed of light really screams out to be recognized as a signal of the fundamental unit of universal construction.) Now, let us consider matter traveling much slower through space. While traveling slowly through the three dimensions of space, matter diverts a significant portion of its energy equivalence to travel through the dimension of time. In essence, pure energy and solid rock both travel at the speed of light but they split their energy equivalence differently among the set of 4 dimensions of our spacetime. Greene describes an analogy as a drag racing car that tends to slant to the right, drifting away from the shortest straight line toward the finish. By diverting some of its motion into a second dimension, the drag racer actually slows its apparent speed in the single dimension that determines a winner of the race. That drag racer might be traveling at the same actual velocity as the winner, but it has spread that actual velocity among more than one dimension. Spreading of actual velocity among more than one dimension caused that drag racer to appear to have traveled at a slower speed than the winner. Now, here is the physical meaning behind that analogy. While light travels quickly through space and not at all through time, matter travels slowly through space while constantly marching through the dimension of time. However, both light and rock travel at the speed of light when considering the total velocity across all dimensions of spacetime.

At first, that small nuance might seem to have no bearing on the topic of the interface between science and faith. However, upon further reflection, this nuance reinforced a deeper understanding of the reality of light as the raw material for this universe. Even further reflection proves relevant to my personal faith in salvation through Jesus Christ. Dr. Greene teaches that all things of this universe really do share the energy equivalence of Einstein's light. Material things expend a significant fraction of their light-energy equivalence traveling through the dimension of time while traveling very slowly through the dimensions of space but still we share the same energy equivalence as light. We really are products of Einstein's light. However, as products born into this realm made from Einstein's slow light, we are trapped in this realm.

We are trapped here, and 'here' is not paradise. I seek a way out of here. **Jesus Christ is that way out, both theologically and physically.** The idea that Christ is 'the light,' and 'the way' may be much more than theological poetry. I'll expand on that thought soon.

I originally studied science as a way to make a living. However, the details of my work involve only a small fraction of the full breadth of the sciences. Beyond that relatively narrow focus, I continue to study the broader scope of the sciences partly through review of the popularized summaries which help bring the sciences to everyone, including those who make a living through other pursuits. I continue to study the sciences and recommend the review of popularized science reviews for others because I find that observations of this natural world consistently reveal the handiwork of God. When pursued with receptivity to the possibility of God, the observation of nature through science reinforces faith. As I learn more about this world I cannot escape this realization:

"My God, this is real! God is absolutely real!

The reality of God is absolutely, unmistakably on display through truthful observations of nature. Natural intelligence represents one palpable sign of our Creator. 'Palpable' was used in the prior sentence for good reason. In this physical realm, the reality of God is not always easy to perceive. I will expand on that thought soon. For now, suffice to say that the study of God's creation helps me **feel** the ambient presence of God in a concrete, tactile way.

'Intelligence' was mentioned in a prior statement for good reason as well. The formal study of intelligence within nature actually represents the next frontier of science and the early yield of this research is driving the atheists crazy! The first chapter of this book described the antagonism directed toward evidence that biological information is statistically different from that expected from the strictly atheistic interpretation of this world. A truly secular scientist should not really care whether there is a God or not, but many do care. Atheists object vigorously to the concept of God. Atheists object because they are primarily committed to the active opposition against God. The hysterical response to the work of Stephen Meyer shows scientific leaders to be anti-theists first, scientists second (see Chapter 1, Atheism Is On the Attack).

It is important to understand that atheism has completely lost the argument about whether this universe was created or not. Their only remaining argument depends upon whether intelligence is or is not a secondary product of organized matter. According to the atheistic view, greater levels of intelligence must be correlated with more complex matter. In the atheist worldview, matter assembles through mechanisms that do not involve God and then intelligence unfolds as a byproduct of the fortunate organization of that matter. To the atheist, humans are more intelligent than earthworms simply because we enjoy a larger and more intricate structure of brain. Intelligence that is primary, not secondary to a structure of matter, is terribly threatening to the atheistic worldview.

The fact that humans can conceive and execute projects like the WMAP satellite is evidence that complex intelligence exists. Which came first, the matter or the intelligence? The faithful believe that intelligence came first. Atheists must disagree. The atheistic premise depends upon a finding that intelligence is always a secondary product of the intricate structure of matter. The problem for the atheist is that measurements of the natural world are not yielding the expected results. Early studies of natural intelligence show a pattern that is statistically different from that expected from the atheistic worldview. Measurements of natural intelligence are showing that intelligence is not a secondary product of organized matter.

I have previously mentioned the work of Francis Collins, author of The Language of God[54]. I suggest this book to all. (It can be enjoyed casually through audiobook format and this is a book that may be better to hear first and read second.). Dr. Collins led the project to map the human genome, a project in biology on par with the landing of a man on the moon. His credentials are simply not subject to challenge. He is a scientist's scientist. Dr. Collins has concluded that the information coded into DNA reflects a complexity that does not support a conclusion that the material structure of DNA matter is primary.

---

[54] Collins, Francis S. The Language of God. A Scientist Presents Evidence for Belief. Free Press, New York, 2006 ISBN 9780743286398

Intelligence demonstrated within the coded information programmed into DNA represents a prerequisite for DNA structure, not a secondary feature of its structure. Even if DNA could self-assemble, the next questions become, "Why did the information encoded by DNA become defined? Why did that information reflect intelligence, even genius?" Of greater importance than the biochemistry for polymer-strand assembly, Dr. Collins recognizes that the real question is how the information behind the biological programming code came to exist. He has become absolutely convinced that the information represents forethought, purposeful intention, which is not the secondary result of the material structure. To the expert in DNA, intelligence clearly came first and biochemistry followed. From the work of Dr. Collins and others, we can now say:

Intelligence is; therefore, God could be.

Atheists just hate that! None-the-less, it is true.

In his book, Dr. Collins summarizes the ways in which his clinical and basic research in medical genetics reinforced his conversion from life-long atheist to a vocal proponent of Christianity. He progresses with ideas that will help many see that opposition to the truthful execution of science is not needed, is not helpful, and is actually harmful to faith. His book will help many who have difficulty dealing with the topic of evolution.

Dr. Collins' work provides direct refutation of the arguments of the atheists but it also refutes the arguments of those who believe that evolution played no role in the handiwork of God. The truth is that the genetic code for humans is completely linked with that of prior life. It is impossible to deny that evolutionary adaptation of physical form is one of God's mechanisms for supporting biological diversity. One might argue that physical fossil evidence skips over key links, but the genetic links are not plagued by gaps.

The good news for fundamentalists is that the study of natural intelligence provides another example in which science reinforces faith. The bad news for some fundamentalists is that evolution as a mechanism for biological diversity is real. Evolution is the mechanism of action through which God brought about biological diversity. This is as certain as the fact that the earth orbits the sun.

When God breathed life into clay, that clay was already alive in the form of a very advanced mammal, a primate. Still, God 'breathed' the human soul into a material construct that was 'from dust' and destined to 'return to dust.' In that sense, our human bodies are inextricably linked to a formation of 'clay,' the term selected from the limited written vocabulary of the ancient Hebrews.

Some of the faithful have engaged in regulatory and legislative warfare against the idea of evolution under the mistaken belief that evolution and creation are incompatible. Dr. Collins does a great job of showing that they are not. The teaching of evolution as a mechanism supporting biodiversity is not wrong. What is wrong is the atheistic editorial that evolution demonstrates the absence of God. Evolution does not demonstrate the absence of God.

Author's Political Digression

Evolution does not disprove God and government funded schools must stop misleading our students in that respect. Government funded educators should be opposed in every instance in which the teaching of science is used as a foundation for propaganda opposed to faith in God.

That said, the tactics used in the past have failed and will continue to fail unless changed. To this point, the faithful have consistently attempted to declare that which the government must teach. That caused the faith community to consistently inherit the role of defendant. As defendant, the faithful will always lose.

We need to stop filling the role of the defendant and start filling the role of the plaintiff. This can be achieved by avoiding attempts to legislate the details of what the government must teach and **begin litigating that which the government cannot teach**. The government cannot teach our children that science conflicts with faith. Our government cannot teach atheism. Our government cannot teach that evolution proceeded in the absence of God.

The book, <u>A Universe from Nothing,</u> discussed in the previous chapter will help illustrate a couple examples of the expansion and reinforcement of faith made possible through a deeper understanding of science.

In the opening chapters of this book, I introduced the concept that 'Energy is, therefore God could be.' I tried to be careful to explain that this does mean that God is simply the energy that we measure with a voltmeter. As big as the pool of energy in this spacetime is, God is even bigger. Creation is not simply the embodiment of God as mischaracterized by the pagan belief of pantheism. God did not make this world by budding Himself off like a yeast. God made this world from nothing, through the exercise of His wisdom. The faithful have taught this as a central tenet of faith for thousands of years. Now the modern scientist can calculate mathematical details consistent with that act of creation. Even though <u>A Universe from Nothing</u> was presented by an atheist in the hopes of supporting atheistic misdirection, we should not lose the opportunity to enjoy the truths of nature revealed in this book. This world really is something brought from nothing! Think about what that teaches!

This world really is something made through the purposeful rearrangement of nothing. This shows the reality of *creatio ex nihilo!* Our ancient ancestors could not have dreamed this up out of thin air. None-the-less they have relayed this cosmic truth through all generations as something taught to early humanity by God. Since antiquity, the faithful have believed in *creatio ex nihilo* because this teaching has been passed down from generation to generation without interruption. Now, Dr. Krauss has been kind enough to do the math. This ancient teaching is true and the study of science lets us see that directly. This is a perfect example of the fact that science and faith are not in conflict. **Truth does not conflict with truth.** God created the earth and the heavens and the scientific study of this world reflects His presence and wisdom as our Creator.

Understanding the reality of creation of all that now exists through the rearrangement of nothing helps refine another topic that I previously discussed. This might be a detail that thrills no one but me, but I am betting that at least one reader will share my experience of a rise of the hairs on the neck. Let me return to the topic of imaginary numbers as plausible coordinates for realms of spacetime that could lie outside our own. Let me specifically address that interesting reality of math called Euler's identity.

"E to the eye pie plus 1 equals zero" is the phonetic verbalization of this famous equation.

$$e^{i\pi} + 1 = 0$$

If you like math, this equation is truly a thing of beauty. This equation blends both imaginary and real numbers to yield a result that would not be expected. One of the truths of imaginary numbers is that a multiplication of any real number by any imaginary number should convert every resulting value into a member of the set of imaginary numbers. However, Euler's equation incorporates an imaginary number (i) into a multiplication that is then used as an exponent, and the result is not an imaginary number. The result is a real number! That oddity explains why great mathematicians have looked at this equation and suggested that it appears to have meaning far beyond the surface. A quote attributed to Benjamin Peirce, a leading 19th century mathematician is roughly paraphrased as, 'I don't get it, but it is proven, so it must mean something.'

I think the mathematical meaning of Euler's identity is a concrete reflection of the fact that zero is the point of mathematical intersection between the set of real numbers and the set of imaginary numbers. However, it could mean more than that. What I present next will be meaningful only to those who are already receptive to God, the Creator of the earth and the heavens, of all that is seen and unseen. It is one of those examples where science does not create faith, but reinforces existing faith.

While reviewing a delightful book gifted to me by a beloved niece and nephew, I came to see this equation in a way that I had never seen before. In his book, Grapes of Math,[55] Alex Bellos presents math in a thoroughly enjoyable way, a way that invites casual reading. Casual is an approach that almost no one takes toward math, but Bellos shows a way. Bellos presents a derivation for Euler's identity that becomes accessible to the average guy, leading this average guy to see Euler's identity in a totally new way.

Just as e=mc^2 is almost always presented in iconic form, I always saw Euler's identify in the iconic form shown below.

$$e^{i\pi} + 1 = 0$$

However, Bellos's derivation of Euler's identity shows rearrangements leading up to that iconic form. These rearrangements broke a box for me. All equations can be rearranged and this one deserves to be rearranged! Having once recognized the following rearrangement, I will never see Euler's equation in any other form. Euler's identity speaks to me as a mathematical herald of the first verses of the Bible.

$$0 = 1 + e^{i\pi}$$

From nothing, God created the tangible and the intangible.

From nothing, God made the simple and the complex, the tangible and intangible, the seen and unseen, the earthly and heavenly (the real number coordinates and imaginary number coordinates).

Centuries ahead of his time, Euler deciphered a mathematical truth showing that real numbers and imaginary numbers can work together. This mathematical truth may have also called out an essential truth regarding creation. We now know that nothing really

---

[55] Bellow, Alex: The Grapes of Math; How Life Reflects Numbers and Numbers Reflect Life New York, Simon & Schuster, 2014. ISBN 978145164009

can be rearranged to yield something. That may be especially practical when nothing emerges as light and a portion of all photons and anti-photons are then separated into more than one realm. The coordinates for one realm might have then become enumerated with real numbers only while one or more other realms became structured using imaginary numbers. I can't say that happened. All I can say is that science knows that this could have happened and this is another example of science remaining consistent with faith in God.

Given the facts of modern science, I think even Victor Stenger would be impressed. The truth is that this world really was created as something out of nothing, and the details of that origin match the 'dangerous prophesy' described more than 3000 years ago by those who believed in the God of Abraham. Understanding the mechanisms through which this world was brought forth and the way it continues to work does not argue against the plausibility of God. Indeed, a detailed understanding of His work through scientific observations helps reveal His presence.

As we study science, we come to understand an important truth, a truth reinforced by the statements of recent Popes. To the distress of some of my Christian brothers, Pope Francis is quoted to have announced, **"God is a Creator, not a magician."** This statement does not reflect a sense of limitation imposed by nature upon God. This reflects a deep understanding of the mechanistic ways through which our Creator has chosen to work. God does not work through instantaneous fiat for every detail. God worked and continues to work by creating a world that operates using physical mechanisms of action, all of which can be traced back to the wisdom of God.

The truth is that science is not the enemy of faith. Science can truthfully reflect that which God has wrought. The truth is that God created the heavens and the earth as described in the Bible. That description is truthfully understood to have taken longer than 6 days starting more than 10,000 years ago. The truth is that biological diversity through mutation and natural selection can represent a valid mechanism through which God develops fundamental forms of life into more advanced forms of life. The truth is that it is wrong to bring the Bible into disrepute because of theological misinterpretation and needless conflict.

Continued opposition to the realities of modern science is not fundamentally different from the errors of my Roman Catholic ancestors who argued that the sun orbited around an earth permanently affixed upon pillars. An important life lesson for all of us is that God's scriptures are simultaneously true and subject to human misinterpretation.

The faithful, all faithful, must recognize that the scriptures reflect the true word of God but are none-the-less difficult to understand. Without intent to insult, I beg my brothers and sisters who fight to support a young-earth theology to consider why they are confident that they possess a superior advantage regarding biblical interpretation compared to any of the rest of God's faithful. How can one feel that they understand without risk of error when even Abraham mistakenly took a second wife because he did not understand God's promise of a son? How can one declare a perfect understanding of God's word when even Moses elected to strike the stone twice instead of once as instructed? How can one declare freedom from error when even Peter could not understand personal, face-to-face instruction until well after the resurrection of Christ? The truth is that God is both real and difficult to understand. This is a truth that we need to acknowledge and deal with together. Working together is the only way to make our way through these difficulties, and perhaps that is a key part of God's plan.

Please consider an idea that might help broaden our shared perspective. Let me point out that the day-age interpretation of Genesis Chapter 1 does not abandon the concept that the scriptures contain literal truth but it accepts the fact that literal messaging is embedded as part of an overall message structured in the form of parable. The parable form is structured to communicate across all generations while the literal detail can only become clear in the fullness of time. As with prophesies of the Old Testament leading to the New Testament, an understanding of the literal versus the allegorical typically requires the passage of many generations. With respect to Genesis Chapter 1, the literal message is not that each step took one current earth-day. The literal truths are that creation was a sequential process, that each step really did take place in its sequence, and that God caused each step. "Let there be light," literally was the first step and the dawn of humanity was the last.

The scriptures always teach truthfully but that does not mean that each generation of mankind is well prepared to understand that which is literal versus that which is allegorical. This is because the concepts taught by the scriptures involve literal detail well beyond the reach of most generations of humanity. God has taught in a way that teaches all generations, even those who lived before the full details could be understood in a literal way. Until the space age, no generation could have possibly understood that light could actually serve as the raw material for clay. Until these most recent decades of the space age, no generation could have any basis for understanding that a division of light could play a literal role in the construction of a cosmos with more than one realm of space and time.

Let me suggest that God is not easy to understand from our perspective because there really is more than one realm of existence and the scriptures reflect truth encompassing all realms of existence. Let me also suggest that one of the reasons God is not easy to understand is that we do not live where we were meant to live. Humanity has literally become swept into a realm that was not our intended fate. For all generations born to a human mother, life is begun and ended within the realm of darkness. This realm of mortal existence is not paradise and birth into this realm has complicated everything.

It is reasonable to interpret the Bible to reflect that the origin of human life was literally located within this cosmos in some preternatural way, a way that allowed humanity to commune functionally with this world while remaining free from the fate of death. This, of course, does not describe our current circumstance.

Science shows that it is possible that separate but adjacent realms such as that described in the parable of Lazarus could be real, not simply a construct of poetic wording. It is possible that the Bible literally reflects a true cosmic structure involving separate realms of existence, with this physical realm not representing paradise in any way. I cannot declare this with absolute certainty, but it is possible that Genesis Chapter 2 reflects a perspective located outside our mortal realm of spacetime. It is plausible that the naming of two rivers known to this world along with two rivers unknown in this world signifies that humanity was originally formed in a realm of existence with coordinates partly shared with this realm and partly not. When the Bible describes the Garden of Eden as paradise, this might not mean a temperate location like the green side of Maui. It is plausible that the paradise of the Bible represents a realm of spacetime not fully enumerated using four real-number coordinates.

It has always been troubling to consider why the sin of only two ancestors transferred culpability to all future generations. Perhaps the reality is that the sin of only two ancestors changed the physical reality for all subsequent generations because it changed the conditions of life. By the action of only two ancestors, all of humanity has inherited a genetic reality of birth through sexual reproduction, complete with the inheritance of all four real-number coordinates for every other animal born through sexual reproduction.

Because of original sin, all subsequent generations of humanity are like victims physically swept into a raging torrent. We are entrapped in a realm of danger, the realm of separation. Could it be that God is not more directly heard, and life is not more easily lived, because our ancestors were tricked into behavior that literally caused all of humanity to be trapped behind enemy lines? Could it be that God did not declare a punishment of man by causing the land that he tilled to be cursed, but that Adam had personally caused a situation in which we must all till the land that had already been cursed as the realm of Satan's separation? Could it be that God did not impose a new punishment upon woman by inflicting increased level of pain during childbirth? Could it be instead that Eve had self-inflicted a situation in which sexual reproduction with painful vaginal birth was the only natural option given the realities of this realm? Could it be that God exclaimed to the woman, "What is this you have done?" not as verbal scolding but as a gasped recognition of the fact that our ancestors had taken actions that would dictate for all subsequent generations a fate of birth, life and death within Satan's realm of darkness. I don't know that these details are certain, but I recognize that human indiscretion doomed all of humanity to a fate from which God immediately set into motion a rescue. The literal existence of more than one realm of spacetime makes this scenario fully possible.

I am not saying that we know for certain that the origin of man took place in a separate realm of spacetime. I am, however, saying that an understanding of the frontiers of science reveals that this is possible. I also am saying that our understanding of the circumstances of human life in relation to our Creator is not hurt by the study of science. Indeed, our understanding of our relationship with our Creator might, in fact, be helped by a solid understanding of science. As we pursue reinforcement of faith, we are helped if we actively embrace all relevant information, including the scientific study of God's creation.

The Scriptures are absolutely the foundation for faith, but Scriptures are not easy to interpret without error. They are best interpreted using collective versus individual interpretation methods.

The truthful study and reflection upon nature provides a source for improving our understanding of God through the physical confirmation of the reality of His work. No single source of truth should be used to the exclusion of the others.

To that point, I would urge that those interested in full understanding of our relationship with God should not reflexively reject the traditional teachings of the early Church. Not every important truth known to the early Church became included into the Bible. Some important truths remain passed down through the generations as faith tradition. These truths are rejected too readily by too many. The fact that the Roman Catholic Church has erred greatly and often since its origins should not cause the faithful to shed the important teachings of ancient tradition. This is especially true since most people forget that early church tradition is not even the product of Roman thought. Early church tradition is the direct product of the Greek Orthodox Church with almost no separation from the experience of Jerusalem. Supplementing the formalized, written scripture with sound Church tradition is important to the pursuit of the whole truth.

Importantly, we need to leave the divisions of the past behind, recognizing that we cannot progress as God has intended without the communal help of others. The reality is that strife between different denominations of the faithful does not represent the greatest risk to faith. Active attack by atheism is today's great risk to faith and to the faithful.

Chapter 10. What Does This Mean to Us?

Even though I am not an elite scientist, my training has been sufficiently broad and deep to understand the interface between science and faith. What I learned is that a person does not need to be a professional in any branch of science to understand the key truths regarding the interface between science and faith. This understanding is within the reach of all of us. Armed with knowledge within the reach of any high school student, we can all recognize that it is patently false for anyone to claim that science argues against the possibility of God. The truth is that science is fully consistent with faith in the communicative, creative God of Genesis Chapter 1. The truth is that God is real!

God is real, but understanding exactly what to do with that information is not a topic on which I claim expertise. I am not a preacher or spiritual advisor. I do not know exactly how to handle everything that life throws at us. All I know for certain is that God is real and is deserving of our loyalty. Translating that into action on any given day is as tough for me as it is for anyone else. With that limitation acknowledged, I will use these closing pages to share thoughts that I have found helpful in consideration of a basis for faith.

Reasons for Faith

I once read an internet posting proposing that the current rate of scientific progress should allow the final disposition of the question of the reality of God within another hundred years or so. That writer portrayed the commonly voiced opinion that God should be considered 'not real' until scientific evidence proves that God is real. That is absolutely unreasonable. That is completely illogical.

Let me be clear on two points. First, the science of the 20th century has already given modern humanity sufficient reason to know that God is plausible. It is a small leap of faith to accept that God is real.

Second, regardless of the status of scientific advancement, the end of life for each individual brings complete personal resolution to any question regarding the reality of God. Do not let life pass without preparing yourself for that day.

Before pursuing a deeper level of faith, one must decide to start trying. Let me invite you to consider that faith can begin with nothing more than receptivity to idea behind the **SETI** project. As vast as this universe is, the **S**earch for **E**xtra**T**errestrial **I**ntelligence is based upon the expectation that intelligent life other than humanity exists somewhere beyond the limits of this planet. Those of faith absolutely believe this premise to be true. However, we recognize that the intelligent life beyond humanity can exist in a form that appears ghostly from our perspective in this spacetime. We believe in the spiritual realm.

Faith begins with the recognition that God is possible and grows upon finding that God is communicative. The Bible is the primary documentation of God's communication with humanity. Through the generations, the divine inspiration of scripture has been taken on faith. Today, modern science confirms that the opening chapter of the Bible is absolutely on target. The balance of these scriptures are also on target, even if they are not always easy to understand.

Today, humanity enjoys more reason to believe in God than that enjoyed by almost any prior generation. We have been given the advantage of scientific confirmation of the truths revealed in these scriptures.

- The universe did have a beginning. *Check.*
- Light was the first step. *Check*
- The balance of steps through the formation of the Sun-Earth-Moon system matches the sequence itemized in 3000 year old records. *Check, check.*
- The sequence of the appearance of life matches those ancient scriptures. *Check, check, check.*

Modern humanity has been given the opportunity to literally and physically probe the opening verses of the Bible and it all checks out. In this modern age of science we have good reasons to believe in the God of the ancient Hebrews.

Genesis Chapter 1 reflects an example of communication from an intelligence that cannot be attributed to humans. These ancient scriptures cannot be claimed to represent the invention of prescientific humanity because they demonstrate advance awareness of highly sophisticated cosmic truths. The modern confirmation of these ancient scriptures cannot possibly be attributed to intentional self-fulfillment by modern humans. While SETI continues its unsuccessful search for intelligent material life, the opening verses of the Bible clearly document intelligent communication from beyond humanity.

God has revealed his presence to humanity through the scriptures but that is not the only demonstration of a communicative God. God also reveals himself to the individual in response to prayer. However, this personal communication is never of a type that can convince anyone except another individual who also prays. While the insincere opponent to God will never measure the impact of prayer, those of us suffering the human reality of receptivity coupled with doubt can expect personal reinforcement of faith in response to sincere prayer.

To the idea of personal religious experience, the skeptic consistently argues that "This claim is just incredible, completely unbelievable. Prayer is entirely self-fulfilling." I can appreciate that challenge, but it is completely off the mark. God will not be tested through the insincere mechanism of a double-blind controlled study. He will not be put to the test by those who oppose Him. This can be debated at length by those fully opposed to God, but I don't need to address the needs of the full blown antagonist. I'm not addressing the full blown atheist right now. Right now, I'm addressing you.

If you wish to sense faith in a more personal way, pray. Pray sincerely. Think, intentionally, of your wish for God's reinforcement of faith. Ask for that which you know has been granted to others. Wealth, health, and other forms of well-being in this world cannot be expected, but you can expect that prayers for reinforcement of faith will be granted. Be patient and pray often. Trust that your faith will be reinforced in ways that dispel all doubt that your Creator is real. You will be given reason to know that God is real and that He is fully aware of you. Expect that this reinforcement will constitute proof for no one but you. Ridicule will be your reward for sharing your details with any except those who also pray in this way.

I can hack ridicule so I will share an experience. My religious upbringing was as a Roman Catholic, a denomination not known for charismatic exuberance. I needed to change high schools at the beginning of my senior year and this change introduced me to a tightly knit group of protestant students. These young men and women were self-described 'Jesus freaks,' fervent adopters of a non-denominational charismatic movement of that time. They were unembarrassed by open expression of faith, even in the face of derision from others. I did not fully join their group but conversed several times. I could not help but marvel at the strength and sincerity of their conviction. Their experience of faith was a source of personal joy, not a duty of performance. I remember praying in private, keeping this group at the forefront of my thoughts. I prayed for a reason to feel faith with the same strength demonstrated by these young men and women. I did not receive a quick response. The responses I have received have not been spectacular; they have not been miraculous. Details will add nothing, but I share witness to the truth that God is real and personally communicative. He does hear personal prayer. He responds to sincere personal prayer. You cannot expect wealth, health, or enhanced physical comfort, but you can trust that God will communicate in a way that is specific to your personal circumstance. If you ask, you will receive God's reinforcement of faith.

Obstacles to Faith – Why is God So Silent?

Although I provide witness to the real presence of a communicative God, I also share the reality that God appears silent almost every hour of every day of life. Those occasional snippets of communication that reinforce faith are neither so frequent nor explicit as to eliminate the very unpleasant challenges of daily life. Life in this world is inescapably linked to frequent experiences of unfairness and profound physical and emotional suffering. Good people suffer undeserved pain. Babies get sick and many die young. The righteous do not reliably come out on top in the struggle for distribution of the physical comforts of this world. These painful experiences cause many to question the reality of God. Even for the faithful, it is easy to wonder, "What is this all about? What is with all this suffering and death? How is that reflective of the love of God?"

I sure wish I knew the full answers to these challenging questions. I don't. However, I know the fundamentals and I know these answers are tied to that great disruption of cosmic peace initiated through the rebellion of Satan. Before closing this work, it is important to consider a reality introduced in Genesis Chapter 2. As surely as this world had a beginning, we can trust that humans were originally destined for life in a realm of existence different from that in which we now live and die.

> The LORD God therefore banished him from the garden of Eden, to till the ground from which he had been taken. He expelled the man, stationing the cherubim and the fiery revolving sword east of the garden of Eden, to guard the way to the tree of life. Genesis 3: 23-24

We were originally fated to live in paradise. We do not currently live in paradise. It is easy to overlook the importance of the teaching that we were intended for life in a different realm, a better realm than that in which we struggle today.

I think it is absolutely mistaken to view the Garden of Eden as simply a unique patch of Earth, or as this planet during some previous day or time. No place on this earth has ever been paradise. No place on this earth was ever free from the ravages of death. It is impossible to believe in God without also understanding that we were originally destined for life in a realm free from the ravages of death and this is not that realm. Where we live now is the realm of death, a realm of separation from God, a realm ruled by the prince of darkness, the author of death.

> And now I have told you before it come to pass, that, when it is come to pass, you might believe. Hereafter I will not talk much with you: **for the prince of this world cometh, and has nothing in me**. John 14:29-30

This is one aspect of scripture that deserves to be read literally. This literal truth explains a lot. This truth explains why everything is much more complicated than it was intended to be. Our birth into this realm of separation complicates our link to God and explains why His presence is not more explicit. In this realm of separation, we are more likely to hear the voice of Satan than the voice of God. We are subjected to very real physical and situational problems inflicted through the efforts of Satan, God's great adversary. Within this realm of darkness, God cannot stop it all and He cannot protect us fully. He needs us to do our part to power through the challenges we face.

Yes, within this realm, God cannot control all things! That adds fuel to the foolish challenge that. 'God is not *all* powerful, therefore God cannot be.' That style of argument, a favorite of Stenger, targets the adjective as a false argument against God. Don't let a linguistic argument against adjectives derail your understanding of the reality of God. God may not be 'all powerful' enough to prevent the disruption and pain inflicted by His opponents, but **God is powerful enough to emerge as the winner!**

You and I face a serious conundrum. As physical products of Einstein's light, the nature of our birth physically entraps us within this realm of darkness. We live each day in a realm of spacetime where the voice of darkness is more vivid than the voice of God. As humans trapped in this realm by the nature of our physical birth, God cannot protect us from all the flaws of this realm. However, entrapment within this realm need not be our long-term fate. We can trust in complete rescue after this material life is complete. In the interim, prayer shifts the balance back in our favor.

For further reading on the topic of the silence of God, I would recommend the excellent work of Philip Yancey, <u>Disappointment with God</u>.[56]

Obstacles – Why is Scripture Difficult to Interpret?

You may have spent many years dismissing scriptures because they are difficult to interpret. You may have considered scriptures to be unreliable because of conflicts between science and incorrect interpretations of the scriptures. The truth is that humans have demonstrated imperfection with respect to our ability to interpret scripture. This is not simply a flaw of medieval Catholics. This imperfection is shared by modern-day fundamentalists as well. However, the imperfection of human interpretation of scripture does not actually cast doubt on the truthfulness of the scriptures themselves. Human error actually demonstrates a level of insulation between the scriptures and intentional human self-fulfillment. We know that humans have not orchestrated a false match between science and scripture. This match has come about through the fact that truth always reflects truth.

---

[56] Yancey, Philip. <u>Disappointment with God</u> Grand Rapids, MI., Zondervan, 1988. ISBN 9780310214366.

Genesis Chapter 1 reflects truth, and the knowledge of this truth originates from beyond humanity. With an understanding of the reality the truthfulness of Genesis Chapter 1 comes the basis for trusting that the rest of biblical teachings are also real. That does not mean that every word is to be read with direct literal meaning, but it does mean that the message behind the words reveals absolute cosmic truth.

> It might not be a literal fact that Noah built a boat capable of housing every type of animal, but it is true that all modern humans are descended from a very small subset of ancient humanity, the only survivors of an event of near extinction. Whether we are descendants of the survivors of a flood or some other catastrophic event, every modern human shares a highly restricted DNA pool reflecting survival and reproduction of a small fraction of the original population of hominids. Avoiding the needless squabble over the detailed definition of a cubit, the story of Noah is another demonstration of advanced knowledge by the ancients of facts that would ultimately be confirmed by modern science.

Starting with Genesis Chapter 1, there is good reason to understand that God is real even if every chapter and verse of the Bible is not easy to understand. This is especially relevant when we understand that every chapter and verse does not apply to humanity at every stage of development. The study of scripture is an exercise in interpretation and it requires a perspective spanning the full history of human development. It is important to appreciate that people needed different methods of teaching and leadership based upon the level of progress toward modernity. The truth is that these scriptures were recorded in writing about 3000 years ago, but can be tracked back through oral tradition to more ancient times. These scriptures reflect the interaction between God and humanity dating back to a time when interbreeding between Homo sapiens and Neanderthal was a reality. These scriptures represent messaging that helped bring humanity through all stages of progress, including learning to cook our kill (burnt offerings), learning to not engage in human sacrifice (Abraham stopped from offering Isaac), and learning to wash before meals long before we understood germ theory (Mosaic Law). These scriptures have recorded ancient teachings that helped ancient humanity progress toward that which we are today. These scriptures have introduced truth through the use of allegory partly because the scriptures demonstrate the communication between God and all generations of humanity. That includes primitive humanity facing realities of survival that one trained in the use of flush toilets simply cannot fathom.

Especially when reading the Old Testament, it is important to understand the role of these scriptures in advancing humanity from primitive to modern stages of development. Frankly, much of the bickering regarding scriptural interpretation involves Old Testament detail that has long since lost its importance for recognizing what God asks of us today. Frankly, the details of the Noah's survival are not as important as the overall message of Noah's survival. This reveals ancient knowledge of the fact that modern humans are all descendants of survivors of a true calamity that eliminated all but a very small band of Homo sapiens. Today, the answers to the greatest questions facing most of modern humanity are not found in the details of the Old Testament. What is important today is to understand what is wanted from us in this age. Most importantly, the question really is "What does God want from me?" not "What does God want me to demand of others? The answer to the questions of modern life will be found in the New Testament, and the answers are not terribly complex.

Obstacles – Why Are Religions Failing So Badly?

You may have spent years dismissing faith because organized religions have failed to meet your expectations for sincerity. There is real truth behind that concern but the arguments of today's militant atheists exaggerate the flaws of organized religion. By portraying historical acts against the modern norms of civics and by generalizing instances of specific crimes as evidence of guilt among all, the modern atheist greatly exaggerate the failures of organized religion. Understanding the whole truth requires recognition that a focus on the flaws of religion at any given time in history is to study a snapshot of humanity at that time. To study the flaws of religion today is to study our collective society today. It is as though religion is nothing more than the result of the efforts of imperfect humans pursuing a goal while still trapped within this realm of darkness. And with that, the truth of our circumstance becomes clear.

Religions reflect the activity of imperfect humans, and humans remain imperfect even when trying to do the right thing. I recognize problems with the clergy, Roman and others. However, I also recognize that the clergy of any generation is simply a subset of the whole population. The clergy is that subset of all of us who volunteer for tough duty at the front lines of the struggle against darkness. Volunteering for religious duty does not suddenly remove the challenges faced by other humans. Indeed there is every reason to expect that the intensity of the challenge is amplified.

There are few instances of failure of the clergy that do not involve complicity from among the rest of us. Today's practice of "drop-off and see-you-later" programs for youth and of inappropriate degrees of personal familiarity from within the laity set the stage for circumstances that can be avoided. The best way to ensure that clergy meet your standards is to become and remain fully engaged in the group activities of the Church. Ensure that clergy enjoy full communal support. Avoid presentation of circumstances that lead away from full communal reinforcement. Life is full of 'tisk-tisk moments.' This is especially true for those who only look on from a distance.

Steps to Engage

Do not shun organized religion, but also do not feel as though you are locked into any single denomination because of the history of your upbringing. Search for a community that meets your needs. At first, you might simply find someone who shares your pursuit toward faith and continue that pursuit together. From there, you may find yourself more engaged in improving the positive aspects of religion than you once thought plausible. I do not steer you in the direction of any specific denomination, though I expect that you will ultimately find both love and wisdom in the choices of your good mother. Personally, I trust that Roman Catholicism is capable of righting itself and remains headed in the right direction more often than not. I join Pope Francis in describing myself as a son of this Church but recognize that this will not be the right choice for many. The most important thing to pursue is community with people who you know and trust. Reach out and find others who share your pursuit. You will find that they help you and many will find that you help them.

If you really do not know where to turn or how to start, let me recommend that you read Timothy Keller, author of The Reason for God: Belief in an Age of Skepticism.[57] Reverend Keller is a Presbyterian teacher who does not water down faith to attract a crowd. He doesn't need to because his way of teaching is absolutely compelling. He is one of many good preachers who know that religion is about determining what God wants from you, not what God wants you to demand from others. Let me also invite you to visit an Episcopal Church, because I think the Episcopal Church represents today's most openly receptive form of Eucharistic Catholicism. (Catholic churches are not limited to Roman Catholicism, but include all of those with worship centered on the literal importance of the Eucharist. Through faithful obedience to His instruction to break bread as He taught, we trust that Christ literally fulfills His promise to be present with us, literally in communion with us.) Regardless of which denomination fits you, seek a church. Find one that shares coffee and a donut. The worst that happens is that you have a bad cup of coffee. (It's hard to find a bad donut.)

To begin, or extend, one's personal journey through faith, it is not critical to understand everything. Just as is the case with science, it is

---

[57] Keller, Timothy. The Reason for God: Belief in an Age of Skepticism. New York, Dutton, 2008 ISBN 9781594483493

not important to personally understand it all. It is just important to be interested in understanding more. That is enough to initiate the journey toward a more complete understanding. Do not let the complexity of the full set of scriptures stop your pursuit of deeper faith. Do not let the imperfections of organized religion stop that pursuit either. There is enough confirmed truth in the Bible to justify the pursuit of a deeper faith and there are enough good people out there to help us all take those important next steps. Do not let the apparent silence of God stop your progress. Pray for reinforcement of faith, and expect that such prayers will certainly be answered.

This book has shown that the Bible begins by revealing cosmic truth about the origin of our world. Genesis Chapter 1 describes the process of formation of this world from nothing. Modern science fully confirms the process as described in those ancient scriptures. Think deeply about what that means. That means that our Creator is real! God is real!

It is logical and reasonable to live in recognition of the reality of God. Become receptive to that reality. Open your mind and open your heart. Pursue faith through sincere prayer. Through prayer, ask what is expected from you. Expect that the answer to your prayers will most likely not be spectacular. The response will not be as clear as ink on paper. Most likely a paraphrase of God's answer will be something like, "Believe in Me. Follow Me. Live your life in a way that demonstrates that you will make a good citizen in My kingdom. Defer to Me. Let Me be the boss. You will find that I am a good boss." For most of us, the demand from God for a life well-lived really doesn't get more challenging than that.

The greatest question of life boils down to this. **With which side of the great cosmic struggle do I align?** That question is very binary. There is no middle ground. To frame your answer, think about these questions. Give yourself the advantage of your best logic and your sharpest reasoning.

- Does humanity really embody the best and brightest mind this universe has to offer?
- Are my thoughts and feelings really just the result of biochemistry?
- When my body dies, does my mind die with it?
- Isn't it possible that intelligent life in a form like pure energy could be more real than intelligence as the fleeting byproduct of material structure?

Know this. Science does not present even the slightest evidence against the plausibility of God. You may choose to not embrace loyalty to God, but you cannot claim that the facts of science forced that choice upon you. That choice is yours alone. Science teaches no fact that absolves you of a personal duty to choose between loyalty and disloyalty.

Your choice of loyalty versus disloyalty is not absolutely final until you draw your last breath, but realize that the way you choose to live now says a lot about how your thoughts will flow at the time of that last breath. As you decide whether, and how, to move forward, keep in mind that we are physical constructs of Einstein's slow light. As such, we are literally trapped within this realm of spacetime. Then think about faith in God from a slightly different perspective. As you look at this world, do you think that evil is real? The more I have reflected on our circumstance, the more I have become convinced that evil is real in this spacetime. I have become convinced that I want out of this place. Fortunately, there is a way out.

The scriptures of the New Testament continue to reflect understanding of cosmic reality that could not represent the simple creativity of human authors (e.g., the reality of more than one realm of existence). I believe that Jesus Christ is as claimed, the human incarnation of Divinity, truly human and truly God. I believe that God became human, just like us, except through a biological mechanism supporting asexual reproduction.

Regarding virgin birth, there is too much detail to be covered fully in the concluding pages of a book focused mainly upon the physical sciences, but suffice to say this. Virgin birth is not any more infeasible than are *in vitro* fertilization or mammalian cloning. Parthenogenesis, the formal term for virgin birth, occurs naturally in vertebrates as advanced as birds but is claimed by atheists to be impossible in humans. However, through manipulation of gene expression in maternal DNA, successful virgin birth has been engineered in the laboratory mouse. Atheists routinely dismiss anything that appears to represent a supernatural miracle, but anyone familiar with *in vitro* fertilization knows that a 'miracle' is not really miraculous when you can literally reach out and touch the right cell correctly. There is every reason to expect that the Maker of our cells can work on the scale of an individual cell with nothing less than the finesse of a human scientist. Parthenogenesis has now been documented in the laboratory mouse, therefore it is scientifically unreasonable to declare that virgin birth in a human maiden is impossible.

The New Testament scriptures teach us that God chose to enter this realm as a true human, born of woman, destined to share our fate of death. He chose this over direct apparition. Why? And why the virgin birth? And why the violent death? If Christ was God, and if the purpose of Christ was the forgiveness of sin, why couldn't forgiveness just be granted by divine fiat?

I think that the incarnation of God was not simply to allow His teaching to take place for a very brief time in a very limited geographical region. No, it was not for that. The incarnation of God was undertaken so that God could engage Satan in a final battle, a direct battle undertaken within Satan's realm. Christ won that battle, and in that victory, gained the release of humanity from Satan's grip without breaching the wall of separation that keeps Satan excluded from the realm of heaven.

Both scripture and church tradition reveal that Christ won our release from this realm, not strictly through His death, but through His life spent free of sin. Christ suffered every challenging experience that any other human has, but never gave into sin. His death completed the first and only human life without sin. Christ was born without original sin. Christ lived as a true human without sin. Death for Christ was a brutal trauma, hideously exaggerated by Satan, but still accepted freely by the One who had not sinned. As a true human, death for Christ provided access to the spiritual realm into which all dead humans had been doomed. However, as a dead human guilty of no sin, Christ was not under Satan's grip. As the superior Being, Christ was able to inflict complete defeat upon the prince of darkness in his own realm. Now, in a way enjoyed by no other, Christ can both enter and leave Satan's realm at will, without limitation, and without reciprocation. Satan remains entrapped in this realm but Christ can come and go as He pleases. Christ can take out of this realm any who ask.

As a person pursues a greater understanding of faith, it becomes impossible to be left unimpressed by the effectiveness and justness of God's mechanism for establishing a heavenly realm of perfect goodness. Heaven is a realm of perfection established by separating all that is good from all that is not. Allowing that separation to be guided by the choice of the individual makes the basis for that separation perfectly fair. Many people mistakenly interpret the concept of hell as a realm of divine punishment. Hell may be an experience of torment, but it is not torment directly inflicted by God. God enforces separation as the practical mechanism for purification of all that is good. Hell is the practical byproduct of purification through separation. A prison building, a place of separation, is not inherently brutal. However, the behavior of inmates can make any prison a brutal realm of torment. The torment associated with hell is not an infliction meted out by God, but the striking out of openly evil inmates.

God's mechanism for gaining a perfected empathy for those who are judged is truly brilliant. God became one of us, not an apparition, but a true human made of mortal flesh. Through His life as a human, Christ endured the experience of humanity in ways that allow Him to understand you and I with perfect empathy. He knows the challenges of the flesh, but still prevailed in the face of the worst set of challenges that Satan can inflict upon any human. There is nothing that we have experienced that Christ cannot personally understand. He chose to come here and do this, yet does not judge as the master who outperformed us all. He judges as one with perfect compassion for our circumstance. He understands that we cannot rival His accomplishments. He understands that we cannot earn our way into heaven. Our access into heaven is not earned, but granted as a gift. All we need do is ask.

Christ was born into life as a true human, was killed, was buried, and rose again from the dead. Christ demonstrated the first transformative resurrection consistent with the immortality promised in the afterlife. Christ did not receive the temporary reprise from death granted to Lazarus, the daughter of the centurion, and others. Christ demonstrated the first true resurrection of the body, the achievement of the transformed heavenly state of the immortal body, a body capable of life within the heavenly realm, forever free from death and fully protected from the trauma and pain of Satan's realm of darkness.

Although I cannot develop this topic fully in these closing pages, I recommend that the interested reader study all they can regarding the Shroud of Turin.[58, 59 60]

---

[58] Ruffin, Bernard C. The Shroud of Turin. 1999. Our Sunday Visitor Publishing Division, Our Sunday Visitor, Inc. USA. ISBN 0-87973-617-8 LCCCN:99-70509

[59] http://www.holypictureofjesus.com/ viewed 05.06.17 The photographic negative of the Shroud of Turin yields a photographic positive image, which uniquely displays in full 3D when viewed under the NASA VP-8 image analyzer.

[60] Public Domain Image. Original Image credit: By Dianelos Georgoudis (Own work) [CC BY-SA 3.0 (http://creativecommons.org/licenses/by-sa/3.0)], via Wikimedia Commons. Image enhanced using online software by https://convert.town and http://www.fotor.com

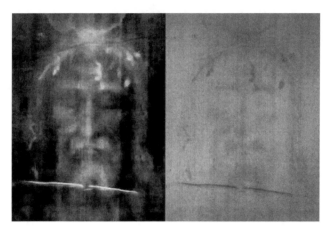

This artifact is either the most amazing piece of work ever created by a human artist, or it is the electrophysical record of the energy dynamics of Christ's resurrection into the first immortal body of the heavenly realm.[61] Either way, the technology incorporated into the production of that image represents another demonstration of knowledge beyond un-coached humanity.

Even to this day, no technologist can reproduce every feature of this work, which includes not a single error in any one of millions of pixels of data. Yes, this old image is created as a collection of pixels encoding not simply an image but a photographic negative of an image. This is not simply a 2-D photographic negative image, but a photographic negative with 3-dimensional data perfectly encoded into its pixel density. This image is like no other image.

This artifact calls out to all, "I am Jesus Christ, God as Man. I have personally taken on the battle against Satan on your behalf. I have overcome Satan's brutality and have defeated the author of death in his realm of darkness. I have done this to secure your release. Will you accept my lead?"

---

[61] Simon Peter, following him, also came up, went into the tomb, saw the linen cloth lying on the ground, and also the cloth that had been over his head; this was not with the linen cloth but rolled up in a place by itself. (John 20:6-7).

With or without that Shroud, those who pursue a reinforcement of faith will come to understand that Christ really is the truth. He really is our way out of this place. He is our only way out of this place.

That said, it is reasonable to expect that Christ will chose to save many who are not Christian. Contrary to some dogmatists, it is important to recognize that Christ never focused on church affiliation but focused always on behavior. He was highly critical of the Pharisees, the overly formal religious elite of that age. Christ most often reached across lines of division, reaching out to those thought unworthy by the elite of that age (Samaritans, lepers, tax collectors, and prostitutes were dearly welcomed). Pope Francis has voiced the ever more common expectation that Christ judges the qualities of each individual, member of a formalized Christian denomination or not. We can expect that every human soul is the recipient of the gift of personal judgment by Christ. We can expect that this judgment for every person will involve perfect empathy for the individual, with a perfect understanding of the circumstances of life faced by each person. We can trust that Christ alone will judge correctly and compassionately based upon each individual's circumstance.

That judgment will be based upon Christ's assessment of whether the person demonstrated, in life, the characteristics of one who wants to accept the role of loyal and peaceful citizen in the Kingdom of God. We can expect that some who self-identify as agnostic will make it to heaven while a proportion of all priests and other faithful will not. In the long run, salvation is a matter of the heart. Salvation is determined by your capacity to love others and your willingness to accept the sovereignty of God.

In defense of the dogmatists, I agree that Christ makes clear that those who believe in Him will find salvation. That can be taken as absolute truth. Although many non-Christians will be saved, the most assured way to receive Christ's gift of salvation from this realm of darkness is to ask for it. Believe in Christ and ask for His help. Follow His teachings which you will find to be not hard. In paraphrase, they go like this.

Know that God is real. Live as though that means something to you. It does. It means that everything can work out right. Live in the pursuit of a better understanding of God. Scripture helps. Prayer helps. Community helps.

Know that those around you are important. Take a look at those around you. Ask whether there is anything you can do to make their life better. Do what you can to make that happen. Take joy from that.

Know that you are valued. Indeed you are invited to join into full communion with your Creator.[62] You will be given every chance to accept God's invitation to join those of peace. Understand that the challenges of this realm are fleeting. Trust that the answers for all of life's challenges are found somewhere in the two prior paragraphs. Live life according to the paraphrased words of Pope Francis:

> Even though life is not free from troubles, live as though you know the hope of Christ. Trust that God promised us life in a world made new. Know that our most beautiful days are still to come. We are a people more of spring than autumn. [63]

In the fullness of time, when it comes time to accept death, embrace death for what it is. Death in this realm can represent true birth into a new realm, the realm of perfected peace. Live in pursuit of that goal. Ask for the rescue offered through Jesus Christ. Approach the last breath of life in this realm without fear because you are about to meet your maker, your King, your way home. That is the promise and reward of faith.

---

[62] Gaudium et Spes, Pastoral Constitution on the Church in the Modern World Second Vatican Council, 1965

[63] For Christians, life always has meaning, even when it's hard. Pope Francis, public address, Aug 23, 2017. Catholic News Agency

Appendix 1. Biblical Accounts of Our Origin

Genesis Chapter 1 [64]

1 In the beginning, when God created the heavens and the earth[65]

2 and the earth was without form or shape, with darkness over the abyss and a mighty wind sweeping over the waters—

3 Then God said: Let there be light, and there was light.

4 God saw that the light was good. God then separated the light from the darkness.

5 God called the light "day," and the darkness he called "night." Evening came, and morning followed—the first day.*

6 Then God said: Let there be a dome in the middle of the waters, to separate one body of water from the other.

7 God made the dome,* and it separated the water below the dome from the water above the dome. And so it happened

8 God called the dome "sky." Evening came, and morning followed—the second day.

9 Then God said: Let the water under the sky be gathered into a single basin, so that the dry land may appear. And so it happened: the water under the sky was gathered into its basin, and the dry land appeared

10 God called the dry land "earth," and the basin of water he called "sea." God saw that it was good.

11 Then God said: Let the earth bring forth vegetation: every kind of plant that bears seed and every kind of fruit tree on earth that bears fruit with its seed in it. And so it happened:

12 the earth brought forth vegetation: every kind of plant that bears seed and every kind of fruit tree that bears fruit with its seed in it. God saw that it was good.

13 Evening came, and morning followed—the third day.

14 Then God said: Let there be lights in the dome of the sky, to separate day from night. Let them mark the seasons, the days and the years

15 and serve as lights in the dome of the sky, to illuminate the earth. And so it happened:

---

[64] http://www.usccb.org/bible/genesis/1

[65] This section, from the Priestly source, functions as an introduction, as ancient stories of the origin of the world (cosmogonies) often did. It introduces the primordial story...Until modern times the first line was always translated, "In the beginning God created the heavens and the earth." Several comparable ancient cosmogonies, discovered in recent times, have a "when...then" construction, confirming the translation "when...then" here as well. "When" introduces the pre-creation state and "then" introduces the creative act affecting that state. The traditional translation, "In the beginning," does not reflect the Hebrew syntax of the clause. Footnote from http://www.usccb.org/bible/genesis/1

16 God made the two great lights, the greater one to govern the day, and the lesser one to govern the night, and the stars'

17 God set them in the dome of the sky, to illuminate the earth,

18 to govern the day and the night, and to separate the light from the darkness. God saw that it was good.

19 Evening came, and morning followed—the fourth day.

20 Then God said: Let the water teem with an abundance of living creatures, and on the earth let birds fly beneath the dome of the sky.

21 God created the great sea monsters and all kinds of crawling living creatures with which the water teems, and all kinds of winged birds. God saw that it was good,

22 and God blessed them, saying: Be fertile, multiply, and fill the water of the seas; and let the birds multiply on the earth

23 Evening came, and morning followed—the fifth day.

24 Then God said: Let the earth bring forth every kind of living creature: tame animals, crawling things, and every kind of wild animal. And so it happened:

25 God made every kind of wild animal, every kind of tame animal, and every kind of thing that crawls on the ground. God saw that it was good.

26 Then God said: Let us make* human beings in our image, after our likeness. Let them have dominion over the fish of the sea, the birds of the air, the tame animals, all the wild animals, and all the creatures that crawl on the earth.

27 God created mankind in his image; in the image of God he created them; male and female* he created them.

28 God blessed them and God said to them: Be fertile and multiply; fill the earth and subdue it.* Have dominion over the fish of the sea, the birds of the air, and all the living things that crawl on the earth.

29 God also said: See, I give you every seed-bearing plant on all the earth and every tree that has seed-bearing fruit on it to be your food;

30 and to all the wild animals, all the birds of the air, and all the living creatures that crawl on the earth, I give all the green plants for food. And so it happened.

31 God looked at everything he had made, and found it very good. Evening came, and morning followed—the sixth day.

Psalm 104 [66]

I

1Bless the LORD, my soul!

    LORD,\

     my God, you are great indeed!

    You are clothed with majesty and splendor,

2 robed in light as with a cloak.

    You spread out the heavens like a tent;

3 setting the beams of your chambers upon the waters.*

    You make the clouds your chariot;

    traveling on the wings of the wind.

4 You make the winds your messengers;

    flaming fire, your ministers.

II

5 You fixed the earth on its foundation,

    so it can never be shaken.

6 The deeps covered it like a garment;

    above the mountains stood the waters.

7 At your rebuke they took flight;

    at the sound of your thunder they fled.

8 They rushed up the mountains, down the valleys

    to the place you had fixed for them.

9 You set a limit they cannot pass;

    never again will they cover the earth.

III

10 You made springs flow in wadies

    that wind among the mountains.

11 They give drink to every beast of the field;

    here wild asses quench their thirst.

12 Beside them the birds of heaven nest;

    among the branches they sing.

13 You water the mountains from your chambers;

    from the fruit of your labor the earth abounds.

14 You make the grass grow for the cattle

    and plants for people's work

    to bring forth food from the earth,

15 wine to gladden their hearts,

    oil to make their faces shine,

    and bread to sustain the human heart.

16 The trees of the LORD drink their fill,

---

[66] HTTP://WWW.USCCB.ORG/BIBLE/PSALMS/104 Viewed 06.14.2015 Permissions per: HTTP://WWW.USCCB.ORG/BIBLE/PERMISSIONS/INDEX.CFM

the cedars of Lebanon, which you planted.

17 There the birds build their nests;
the stork in the junipers, its home.

18 The high mountains are for wild goats;
the rocky cliffs, a refuge for badgers.

IV

19 You made the moon to mark the seasons,
the sun that knows the hour of its setting.

20 You bring darkness and night falls,
then all the animals of the forest wander about.

21 Young lions roar for prey;
they seek their food from God.

22 When the sun rises, they steal away
and settle down in their dens.

23 People go out to their work,
to their labor till evening falls.

V

24 How varied are your works, LORD!
In wisdom you have made them all;
the earth is full of your creatures.

25 There is the sea, great and wide!
It teems with countless beings,
living things both large and small.

26 There ships ply their course
and Leviathan,* whom you formed to play with.

VI

27 All of these look to you
to give them food in due time.

28 When you give it to them, they gather;
when you open your hand, they are well filled.

29 When you hide your face, they panic.
Take away their breath, they perish
and return to the dust.

30 Send forth your spirit, they are created
and you renew the face of the earth.

VII

31 May the glory of the LORD endure forever;
may the LORD be glad in his works!

32 Who looks at the earth and it trembles,
touches the mountains and they smoke!

33 I will sing to the LORD all my life;
I will sing praise to my God while I live.

34 May my meditation be pleasing to him;
I will rejoice in the LORD.

35 May sinners vanish from the earth,
and the wicked be no more.
Bless the LORD, my soul! Hallelujah!*

Appendix 2. Time as a Function of Mass

There are some details worthy of additional attention. One of those details is the actual definition of time. Recall the conundrum voiced by St. Augustine in the 4th century A.D.? While theologically believing that time was something that began with the world and would end with this world, Augustine could not actually describe what time was. To paraphrase Augustine, time is something easily understood until the need arises to describe and explain it.

I suggest that we can now define time using the knowledge of physics available in this early 21st century. Absent matter, time is undefined. With matter, the definition of time remains variably dependent upon the conditions of interaction of energy upon matter. With the reader's indulgence I would ask to extend the discussion of the underlying meaning or definition of time following a line of argument to which I can provide no reference and can provide no data beyond the rearrangement of confirmed equations of physics. This concept could be completely wrong, but it is only a very slight extension of well-established fact.[67]

Let me posit that time is a secondary byproduct, the measurable result of the movement of mass in response to the action of energy. That means that time is not simply measured by the movement of mass, time is created by the movement of mass.

With pure energy, time does not exist. Time has value in real terms only in the presence of mass traveling slower than the speed of light. Absent mass, time is undefined. In the presence of mass, time becomes defined according to the Lorentz-Fitzgerald ratio.

---

[67] Attributed to no known referenced authority; presented as the author's personal assessment with risk that this might be completely wrong

No mass = no time
Some mass = some time
How much time? This depends upon the details of mass.

The amount of time lapsed over any period under study would be the mathematical equivalence of a relationship involving the following primary factors:

1. the total amount of mass moved,
2. the distance over which the mass was moved, and
3. the amount of force exerted to cause the movement.

Basic concepts of the physics known to Newton provide a starting point for seeing a relationship that helps create a mathematical definition of time as a function of the movement of mass. One of Newton's many contributions to the physical sciences was the determination of the relationships that fully describe motion of massive objects as a function of the force acting on the objects. One of his simplest but most useful relations is

$$F = ma \text{ Equation 6}$$

Which is read as:

$$Force = (mass) \; x \; (acceleration)$$

This relationship can be rearranged using basic algebra to find that

$$acceleration = \frac{force}{mass} \text{ Equation 7}$$

As per our personal experience, acceleration goes up when more force is applied to a given mass. Literally, if force is increased by 2-fold, then acceleration is increased by 2-fold. However, with mass in the denominator of this equation, we will find that acceleration becomes less when mass is increased. Literally, if mass is increased by 2-fold while force is unchanged, then acceleration would be only 1/2 of that achieved with a single unit of mass. For hundreds of years, these equations have been used for many practical applications while a fundamental omission of definition went overlooked.

In these famous equations taught by Sir Isaac Newton, **time** is included in the details of various terms as though it was a standard unit of existence, unchanging and without need of further definition. For instance, acceleration is defined as the change in speed over time. Time is not defined by Newton, it is simply used. Speed itself is a parameter that is also dependent upon time. Speed is defined as the change in distance over time. Miles per hour is the common term for speed in the US, but kilometers per second would be a more standardized scientific ratio. Equation 6 and 7 rely upon the term acceleration, which involves time, without any attention to defining what time is. The definition for mass does not involve a presumed value for time, but the definition of force does.

The basic unit of force in the International System of Units (SI) has been named, fittingly, the newton (N). One newton is defined as the force that will accelerate a 1 kilogram mass by 1 meter per second per each second the force is applied. That defining relationship is shown as Equation 8.

$$\{1\ \text{N}\} = 1\ \text{Kg} * 1\frac{\left(\frac{\text{m}}{\text{s}}\right)}{[\text{s}]} \quad \text{Equation 8}$$

This reads from left to right as
- 1 newton
  - equals
- 1 kilogram of mass (the amount of *m, mass*)
  - Times
- one meters-per-second-per second

It is clear that a unit of time (the second) is critical for the function of these equations, but Newton failed to address any detail of the definition of time. None-the-less, his equations work perfectly for making things work in our everyday world. Isaac Newton never enjoyed travel in an automobile, but no automobile could have ever been engineered without his equations. Today it is clear to everyone that if you want a car to reach top speed in less time, you will make a car lighter and provide a more forceful engine.

Attention to these types of details represented the primary goal of clock makers striving to develop more accurate machines for measuring time. Controls to establish a consistent force working against an unchanging resistance led to the development of more consistent time pieces. Now, let us flip around the thought process that led to refinements in clocks. Instead of concluding simply that the steady, consistent movement of mass can measure time, it is plausible to consider the restatement of known relationships. Today, it is reasonable to consider the possibility that the movement of mass actually creates time.

$$\{1 \text{ N}\} = 1 \text{ Kg} * 1 \frac{\left(\frac{\text{m}}{\text{s}}\right)}{[\text{s}]} \quad \text{Equation 8}$$

Look at Equation 8 above. This is the definition of a Newton, the basic unit of force. Note that the units of time (seconds) are simply buried in the details of the right hand side of that equation. However, algebraic rearrangement of that equation will yield a functional definition of the fundamental unit of time (second) as the result of the application of force upon mass over distance.

Consider the rearrangement of Equation 8 to yield Equation 9 below. Notice that the basic unit of time [s] is involved in a division step on the right side of the equation. That allows us to use very simple algebra to move [s] to the left side of the equation. We simply multiply both sides of the equation by [s]. Now {1 N} (one newton) can be rearranged to the right side of the equation by dividing both sides of equation 8 by $\{1 N\}$. With that 7th grade algebraic rearrangement, we get the Equation 9 below.

$$[s] = \frac{\left([1\ Kg]*1\frac{\left(\frac{m}{s}\right)}{1}\right)}{\{1\ N\}} \quad \text{Equation 9}$$

That can be read as

- 1 second in time equals the result of
- 1 kg of mass becoming accelerated to
- the speed of 1 meter per second
- by the exertion of exactly 1 newton of force.

In this rearrangement, we have restated a definition for the 1 second unit of time as the result of the action of a given amount of force upon a given mass. Now this rearrangement provides a relatively intuitive definition of the value of time as a function of the action of force upon energy, but this still involves the use of a measure of time within the right side of the equation. We can move that term from the right to the left side of the equation by multiplying both sides of the equation by S once again. This gives us equation 10.

$$S^2 = \frac{1\ Kg*1\ m}{1\ N} = \quad \text{Equation 10}$$

Since we really are not interested in the value for seconds squared, we will take the square root of both sides to yield Equation 11.

$$S = \sqrt{\frac{1\ Kg*1m}{1\ N}} \quad \text{Equation 11}[68]$$

Under this rearrangement, one second is defined as the square root of 1Kg mass moved 1 meter through the action of 1 newton of force. As would be expected, mass moved a further distance through the

---

[68] Relativistic corrections for this relationship should be inherent with appropriate relativistic correction for Kg, m, and s concurrently applied under all conditions.

action of any given amount of force causes the lapse of more time. As might not have seemed feasible in the time of Newton, movement of less mass yields less time than the movement of more mass. The insertion of a value of zero kilograms for the mass introduces the result expected through the Lorentz-Fitzgerald equations supporting relativity theory. With zero mass, force might act, but zero seconds of time would be measurable.

$$\textbf{0 seconds} = \sqrt{\frac{0\ Kg*1m}{1\ N}} \qquad \text{Per Equation 11}$$

Through established features of relativity theory, we know that time is undefined at the speed of light and we know that only pure energy travels at the speed of light. It is not absurd to conclude that time really is an illusion, the secondary byproduct of the presence and movement of mass. In the absence of matter, time is meaningless.

So, returning to Augustine's difficult question, how could one actually define what time is? This author thinks time can be defined as the measure of cumulative movement of mass. It seems reasonable to teach that the stars of the heavens do not just mark the passage time, they cause time to exist and define the rate at which cosmic time passes.

For those who wonder why the arrow of time always points forward, I propose it is because one can never 'unmove' a moved star. Even the reversal of a pendulum simply adds to the cumulative movement of all cosmic mass. The cosmic arrow of time always points forward because cumulative movement of mass always grows larger.

Appendix 3. Three Catholic Topics

I have made no effort to hide the fact that I was brought up as a Roman Catholic. As an adult, I confirm my continued embrace of Catholicism with full knowledge of our imperfections, both past and present. Recognizing the unique forum afforded by this work, I would add a few personal thoughts on three important topics regarding Catholicism.

I have been surprised that recent internet postings demonstrate a high level of continued hostility and suspicion toward Catholics from within some portions of the Christian community. This includes an amazing frequency of claims that Catholicism is or will be the seat of the antichrist. To that I must say this. While theological details have led to divisions within the Christian community, the truth is that Roman Catholic teaching is in full concordance with main stream Christianity. Our creed is encapsulated in the same Apostles' Creed or Nicene Creed shared broadly throughout Christianity. The allegiance of Catholics toward Christ is complete. The antichrist will not be a force characterized by mistakes made in pursuit of loyalty to Christ. The antichrist will be fully against Christ. Catholics are not at all against Christ. We do not represent the antichrist.

The second topic relates to the great distress voiced by many regarding the Catholic devotion toward Mary, the mother of God. Please understand this. Catholics do not replace or downgrade our worship of Christ through our simultaneous devotion to His mother. We understand that Christ is the Lord and that Mary is not. However, we also know that Mary, the mother of God, intervenes on the behalf of humanity. Christ's first public miracle was the turning of water into wine at the wedding in Cana. By the literal words of the Gospel, we know that this was not a topic to which Christ would have granted attention except through the intervention of Mary. Because of Mary, Christ said, "yes" when He would have otherwise said, "no." Catholics understand that Mary can and will intervene on our behalf as well. The Biblical justification for our devotion includes nothing less than the teaching of John 26-28.

> Standing by the cross of Jesus were his mother and his mother's sister, Mary the wife of Clopas, and Mary of Magdala.
>
> When Jesus saw his mother and the disciple there whom he loved, he said to his mother, "Woman, behold, your son."
>
> Then he said to the disciple, "Behold, your mother." And from that hour the disciple took her into his home.

These were Christ's last instructions before He started to display the final agonies of death. We do not believe that Christ waited until this final moment to consider the details for meeting the worldly needs of his surviving mother. We understand this detail was included in the Gospel because these instructions reflect something much bigger than the attention to shelter for Mother Mary. They reflect a practical gift extended to all of humanity, one more demonstration of Mary's service toward the salvation of all. Mary is given to all of mankind as our heavenly mother. Mary is not our Savior but she does have His ear.

Let us take a moment to share the Catholic prayer toward Mary and ask if you can declare what is so wrong about it.

> Hail Mary, full of Grace, the Lord is with thee.
> Blessed are you among women, and blessed is the fruit of thy womb, Jesus.
> Holy Mary, mother of God, pray for us sinners, now and at the hour of our death.
> Amen.

You will find that this prayer is founded upon the Biblical record of the greeting of Mary by Elizabeth, the mother of John the Baptist. You will find that we ask for the intercession of Mary on our behalf, in life and as we meet death. There is nothing in our devotion to Mary that elevates her to equality with Christ. Mary is not our Savior but we acknowledge Mary's unique role in bringing about our salvation. Unique among all, Mary was selected and agreed to take on all the duties and dangers of the direct fight against Satan as the mother of Christ. Those who understand Revelation 12 understand that the role of this woman in the fight against evil was by no means simple and by no means safe. For the good of all mankind, this challenge was taken up by Mary. She cowered from no danger. She shirked no duty. She retreated from no pain. Now, as the fruit of the last instruction of Christ spoken from His cross, the relationship of mother and child has been gifted not just to one apostle, but to all humanity. Mary has been given, and Mary has accepted, the role of heavenly mother for all. Catholics choose to not ignore those final words, that final gift of Christ. We do not forget the lesson of Cana. We ask that Mary intercede on our behalf, trusting that she will lobby for a "yes," even though we deserve nothing better than "no."

The Eucharist is my last point for discussion in this appendix. Those most likely to fight stubbornly over the literal interpretation of the ancient word, "Yom," are most likely to dismiss the literal importance of details from the most recent of all scriptures, the Gospels of the New Testament. More than once, Christ spoke of His expectation that those who believe in Him will eat His body and drink His blood. This was confusing to all, including His apostles. Finally, Christ made clear that the bread and wine of the sacramental supper were to become His body and blood. After His resurrection, Christ frequently assumed physical form that was not immediately recognized. Only in the breaking of bread did the risen Christ become recognized even to His close apostles. The sacrificial offering of bread and wine is taken very seriously, very literally, by Eucharistic Catholics (not just Roman Catholics, but the Orthodox, Lutheran, Episcopal and others who focus on the literal truth of the Eucharist). Much grievance is voiced regarding the Roman Catholic explanation of the Eucharist as the transubstantiation of bread and wine. I would say this about that. To my Catholic leadership, I would ask reconsideration of the teaching on that subject in the same way that we ask our protestant friends to reconsider the duration of a creation day. In this modern age of perfected molecular analysis, we know with absolute certainty that the consecration of the Eucharist does not bring about a change to the proteinaceous molecular equivalent of flesh and blood. The molecules of the bread and wine are unchanged. That said, I urge my protestant friends to recognize that the consecration of the Eucharist is much more than a symbolic act of remembrance. Through the faithful practice of the Eucharist, we are graced with the very real presence of Christ in our physical space and time. Think of it this way. The original body of Christ, born of the womb, was no more essential to the existential nature of God than is the physical construct of the bread and wine. Yet God became incarnate, assumed a physical presence in our space and time, through His divine presence in the living body and blood of the human, Jesus Christ. Today, Catholics trust that God chooses to become incarnate, truly and fully present in our space and time, through the faithful consecration of bread and wine just as He instructed. If you ever wished to invite Christ into your life, the Eucharist is the practical mechanism through which that invitation is realized. The Eucharist is Christ's gift as the literal mechanism for inviting Christ into full physical communion with you, in your physical space and time. Communion, God's common union with us, is brought about through the Eucharist because Christ said so. Christ literally shares our presence in our physical space and time, and literally chooses to be in us so that we can be in Him.

That is why we kneel at communion. Christ has entered the room!

The one last point that I would make regarding the Eucharist is directed to my very conservative Catholic friends and clergy. Since the early days of the papacy of Francis, there has been a great discussion, turmoil actually, regarding the availability of communion for those who have divorced and remarried. The most conservative voices on this subject are failing to understand the issue of faith and the message of mercy that Pope Francis correctly brings forward. The entire resistance to the granting of communion to those who are in a second marriage is argued as though the central question relates to whether marriage is or isn't dissoluble. However, that is not the central question of this issue. The central question is whether the grant of communion is limited only to those whose sins are invisible to others. Can anyone point to the Biblical instruction through which Christ declared His instruction to "eat my body, and drink my blood" was to be followed only by those publicly judged worthy by the clergy? Church leadership and conservative laity speak and act as though the issue of the worthiness of an individual for communion with God is a matter for judgment by mere humans and declared publicly at the time of communion. On this matter, the Roman Catholic Church could not be more completely mistaken. The Eucharist is not a celebration for the perfect, but an offering of Christ's communion with the faithful sinner.

The Church is correct to teach that Christ addressed divorce and remarriage as a problematic reflection of human imperfection. Christ recognizes that divorce and remarriage is not the best plan for His people. Marriage is not dissoluble. However, remarriage is not the only chronic sin among the faithful. The Eucharist is not a celebration to be shared only among those whose chronic sins are invisible to others.

The truth is that Christ taught of no restriction that should prevent the remarried or any other true-to-life sinner from full communion with Christ through the Eucharist. Regarding the participation in the pursuit of Christ's salvation, the Church must acknowledge the reality of the sinful nature of humanity. Christ does not invite us into communion after we first get our act together. We are invited to get our act together by seeking communion with our savior, Jesus Christ, as He instructed. Christ imposed no preconditions upon this gift. No Church ruling should dare interfere with the communion between Christ and those who ask for His salvation.

This is one of many questions that are best resolved through attention to the many instances in which Christ chose to criticize a particular type of human behavior. Of all human behaviors, the one taken to task most often by Christ is the arrogance of those who act negatively toward others in the misguided sense of moral superiority. Regardless of the issue, the best guide is to recognize that Christ's teaching calls us to regularly ask "What does God want of me?" That question is never correctly phrased as, "What does God want me to demand of others?"

Index

Index

Made in the USA
Las Vegas, NV
10 November 2020